Dearest Poppy

On your

With lots & lots of love from

Aunty Kate

XXX

best loved

hymns, poems & readings

best loved hymns, poems & readings

Compiled by Martin H. Manser

Associate Editor: David H. Pickering

TED SMART

This edition produced for The Book People Ltd, Hall Wood Avenue, Haydock,
St Helens WA11 9UL

Collins
A division of HarperCollins*Publishers*
77–85 Fulham Palace Road, London W6 8JB

www.collins.co.uk

First published in Great Britain in 2004 by HarperCollinsPublishers

A catalogue record for this book is available from the British Library.

ISBN 0 00 774600 8

Printed and bound in Germany

Contents

Introduction

This collection of *Best-loved Hymns and Readings* has been compiled as a resource for personal devotion and also as a reference work. It will be useful for making selections for such services as weddings, Christenings, or funerals. You will find here many favourite and traditional hymns, poems, readings, and extracts from the Bible (e.g., 'Amazing Grace' and Jesus' parable of the good Samaritan), together with less familiar ones (e.g., Shakespeare's 'The quality of mercy is not strained'). Each hymn, reading, poem, etc., is given an introduction which sets its background or gives interesting or helpful information. All the readings are arranged in alphabetical order of title (ignoring 'A' or 'The' at the beginning of a title). For ease of reference there are also indexes at the end of the book to enable you to find a particular item by reference to its first line, its author, its overall theme or, where appropriate, its Bible reference.

These extracts have been compiled in the hope that they will provide inspiration and encouragement both for everyday life and also at times of particular need and on special occasions.

Martin H. Manser

Author Index

Author Index

Author Index

Author Index

Author Index

Index of Bible references

Indes of Bible references

Index of first lines

Index of first lines

Index of first lines

Index of first lines

Index of first lines

Index of first lines

Index of themes

Index of themes

Index of themes

Index of themes

Index of themes

Index of themes

Index of themes

Index of themes

Index of themes

Index of themes

Index of themes

Index of themes

Index of themes

Index of themes

Index of themes

Abide with me

Henry Francis Lyte was vicar of the fishing port of Brixham, Devon, and wrote a number of greatly loved hymns, of which 'Abide with me' is perhaps the most celebrated. He wrote it shortly after his last sermon, knowing that his own death (at the premature age of 54) was imminent, having been diagnosed with tuberculosis.

In 1915 Nurse Edith Cavell famously derived strength from this hymn by singing it in her cell the night before she was executed by a German firing squad. Today it is also a great favourite with crowds at football matches.

The original reference is to Luke 24:29, which runs 'Abide with us, for it is toward evening, and the day is far spent.'

Abide with me! fast falls the eventide,
The darkness deepens; LORD, with me abide!
When other helpers fail, and comforts flee,
Help of the helpless, oh, abide with me!

Swift to its close ebbs out life's little day;
Earth's joys grow dim, its glories pass away;
Change and decay in all around I see:
O Thou, who changest not, abide with me!

I need Thy presence every passing hour;
What but Thy grace can foil the tempter's power?
Who like Thyself my guide and stay can be?
Through cloud and sunshine, Lord, abide with me!

I fear no foe with Thee at hand to bless:
Ills have no weight and tears no bitterness:
Where is death's sting? Where, grave, thy victory?
I triumph still if Thou abide with me.

Hold then Thy cross before my closing eyes!
Shine through the gloom, and point me to the skies!
Heaven's morning breaks, and earth's vain shadows flee:
In life and death, O Lord, abide with me!

Henry Francis Lyte (1793–1847)

Adam and Eve

This passage from Genesis 2:18–24 is sometimes used as a Bible reading at weddings. It illustrates the mutual companionship and interdependence that exist in a marriage relationship.

Then the LORD God said, 'It is not good that the man should be alone; I will make him a helper as his partner.' So out of the ground the LORD God formed every animal of the field and every bird of the air, and brought them to the man to see what he would call them; and whatever the man called each living creature, that was its name. The man gave names to all cattle, and to the birds of the air, and to every animal of the field; but for the man there was not found a helper as his partner. So the LORD God caused a deep sleep to fall upon the man, and he slept; then he took one of his ribs and closed up its place with flesh. And the rib that the LORD God had taken from the man he made into a woman and brought her to the man. Then the man said, 'This at last is bone of my bones and flesh of my flesh; this one shall be called Woman, for out of Man this one was taken.' Therefore a man leaves his father and his mother and clings to his wife, and they become one flesh.

Adonais

Percy Bysshe Shelley's lament for fellow-poet John Keats ranks among his most celebrated poetic works. Written in 1821 in response to the news of Keats's premature death from consumption in Rome, it is often quoted in part or in full at funerals (the extracts below comprise the more famous passages).

Many have commented upon the melancholy prescience of the final stanza in which Shelley describes how his own spirit is 'driven far from the shore': the following year he was himself drowned in a sudden storm while sailing in the bay of Lerici.

Peace, peace! he is not dead, he doth not sleep;
He hath awakened from the dream of life.
'Tis we, who lost in stormy visions, keep
With phantoms an unprofitable strife,
And in mad trance, strike with out spirit's knife
Invulnerable nothings. We decay
Like corpses in a charnel; fear and grief
Convulse us and consume day by day,
And cold hopes swarm like worms within our living clay.

He has outsoared the shadow of our night;
Envy and calumny and hate and pain,
And that unrest which men miscall delight,
Can touch him not and torture not again;
From the contagion of the world's slow stain
He is secure, and now can never mourn
A heart grown cold, a head grown grey in vain;
Nor, when the spirit's self has ceased to burn,
With sparkles ashes load an unlamented urn.

He is made one with Nature; there is heard
His voice in all her music, from the moan
Of thunder to the song of night's sweet bird;
He is a presence to be felt and known
In darkness and in light, from herb and stone,
Spreading itself where'er that Power may move
Which has withdrawn his being to its own;
Which wields the world with never-wearied love,
Sustains it from beneath, and kindles it above.

He is a portion of the loveliness
Which once he made more lovely: he doth bear
His part, while the one Spirit's plastic stress
Sweeps through the dull, dense world, compelling there
All new successions to the forms they wear,
Torturing th' unwilling dross that checks its flight
To its own likeness, as each mass may bear,
And bursting in its beauty and its might
From trees and beasts and men into the Heaven's light.

The One remains, the many change and pass;
Heaven's light for ever shines, Earth's shadows fly;
Life, like a dome of many-coloured glass,
Stains the white radiance of Eternity,
Until Death tramples it to fragments. Die,
If thou wouldst be with that which thou dost seek!
Follow where all is fled! Rome's azure sky,
Flowers, ruins, statues, music, words, are weak
The glory they transfuse with fitting truth to speak.

That Light whose smile kindles the Universe,
That Beauty in which all things work and move,
That Benediction which the eclipsing Curse
Of birth can quench not, that sustaining Love
Which, through the web of being blindly wove
By man and beast and earth and air and sea,
Burns bright or dim, as each are mirrors of
The fire for which all thirst, now beams on me,
Consuming the last clouds of cold mortality.

The breath whose might I have invoked in song
Descends on me; my spirit's bark is driven
Far from the shore, far from the trembling throng
Whose sails were never to the tempest given;
The massy earth and sphered skies are riven!
I am borne darkly, fearfully, afar;
Whilst, burning through the inmost veil of Heaven,
The soul of Adonais, like a star,
Beacons from the abode where the Eternal are.

Percy Bysshe Shelley (1792–1822)

Afterwards

This meditation by the poet and novelist Thomas Hardy upon the way a person might be remembered after they have died remains one of his most popular poetic works. It is sometimes recited at funerals.

When the Present has latched its postern behind my tremulous
stay,
And the May month flaps its glad green leaves like wings,
Delicate-filmed as new-spun silk, will the neighbours say
'He was a man who used to notice such things'?

If it be in the dusk when, like an eyelid's soundless blink,
The dewfall-hawk comes crossing the shades to alight
Upon the wind-warped upland thorn, a gazer may think,
'To him this must have been a familiar sight'.

If I pass during some nocturnal blackness, mothy and warm,
When the hedgehog travels furtively over the lawn,
One may say, 'He strove that such innocent creatures should
come to no harm,
But he could do little for them; and now he is gone'.

If, when hearing that I have been stilled at last, they stand at the
door,
Watching the full-starred heavens that winter sees,
Will this thought rise on those who will meet my face no more,
'He was one who had an eye for such mysteries'?

And will any say when my bell of quittance is heard in the
gloom,
And a crossing breeze cuts a pause in its outrollings,
Till they rise again, as they were a new bell's boom,
'He hears it not now, but used to notice such things'?

Thomas Hardy (1840–1928)

All creatures of our God and King

The words for this famous hymn were based upon lines written by St Francis of Assisi (1182–1226). Legend has it that the first four verses were inspired by the saint's experiences after spending forty nights in a rat-infested hut at San Damiano. The fifth verse supposedly resulted from a quarrel between the church and civil authorities of Assisi, while the sixth stanza was written as the saint endured great suffering on his deathbed.

William Henry Draper, rector of a parish in Yorkshire, subsequently produced his celebrated translation of St Francis's words for a Whitsuntide festival for school children in Leeds. The music was the work of Ralph Vaughan Williams, who based it upon a seventeenth-century tune from Cologne.

All creatures of our God and King,
Lift up your voice and with us sing,
Alleluia, alleluia!
Thou burning sun with golden beam,
Thou silver moon with softer gleam:

O praise Him, O praise Him,
Alleluia, alleluia, alleluia!

Thou rushing wind that art so strong,
Ye clouds that sail in heaven along,
O praise Him, alleluia!
Thou rising morn, in praise rejoice;
Ye lights of evening, find a voice:

Thou flowing water, pure and clear,
Make music for thy Lord to hear,
Alleluia, alleluia!
Thou fire, so masterful and bright,
That givest us both warmth and light:

Dear mother earth, who day by day
Unfoldest blessings on our way,
O praise Him, alleluia!
The flowers and fruits that in thee grow,
Let them His glory also show:

And ye that are of tender heart,
Forgiving others, take your part,
O sing ye, alleluia!
Ye who long pain and sorrow bear,
Praise God, and on Him cast your care:

And thou, most kind and gentle death,
Waiting to hush our latest breath,
O praise Him, alleluia!
Thou leadest home the child of God,
And Christ our Lord the way has trod:

Let all things their creator bless,
And worship Him in humbleness;
O praise Him, alleluia!
Praise, praise the Father, praise the Son,
And praise the Spirit, Three in One:

William Henry Draper (1855–1933)

All people that on earth do dwell

This hymn, published in 1561, is based on Psalm 100 and has therefore come to be popularly dubbed 'The Old Hundredth'. Its author was a Scottish-born minister in the Church of England who fled the country after the accession of the Catholic Queen Mary.

All people that on earth do dwell,
Sing to the Lord with cheerful voice:
Him serve with fear, His praise forth tell;
Come ye before Him and rejoice.

The Lord, ye know, is God indeed;
Without our aid He did us make;
We are His flock, He doth us feed,
And for His sheep He doth us take.

O, enter then His gates with praise,
Approach with joy His courts unto;
Praise, laud, and bless His name always,
For it is seemly so to do.

For why? the Lord our God is good,
His mercy is for ever sure;
His truth at all times firmly stood,
And shall from age to age endure.

William Kethe (d.1594)

All things bright and beautiful

Cecil Frances Alexander was an Irish hymn writer and poet who married William Alexander, Protestant bishop of Derry, in 1850. She bore her husband four children and, among other good deeds, helped her family to establish a school for 'deaf and dumb' children. She wrote some 400 hymns, among them such classics as 'There is a green hill far away' and 'Once in royal David's city'. The original third verse of this hymn, running 'The rich man in his castle, / The poor man at his gate, / God made them, high or lowly, / And ordered their estate', has long since been omitted.

All things bright and beautiful,
All creatures great and small,
All things wise and wonderful,
The Lord God made them all.

Each little flower that opens,
Each little bird that sings,
He made their glowing colours,
He made their tiny wings.

The purple-headed mountain,
The river running by,
The sunset, and the morning
That brightens up the sky:

The cold wind in the winter,
The pleasant summer sun,
The ripe fruits in the garden,
He made them every one.

The tall trees in the greenwood,
The meadows where we play,
The rushes by the water
We gather every day.

He gave us eyes to see them,
And lips that we might tell
How great is God Almighty,
Who has made all things well.

Cecil Frances Alexander (1818–95)

All we like sheep

Isaiah 53, perhaps more than anywhere else in the Old Testament, contains clear prophecy of the sufferings and coming to glory of Jesus Christ. This passage is seen as a description of the 'Suffering Servant', a role that, together with that of the conquering lordship of the expected Messiah, was uniquely fulfilled in Christ.

Handel used this passage in his oratorio, Messiah.

Who hath believed our report? and to whom is the arm of the LORD revealed?

For he shall grow up before him as a tender plant, and as a root out of a dry ground: he hath no form nor comeliness; and when we shall see him, there is no beauty that we should desire him.

He is despised and rejected of men; a man of sorrows, and acquainted with grief: and we hid as it were our faces from him; he was despised, and we esteemed him not.

Surely he hath borne our griefs, and carried our sorrows: yet we did esteem him stricken, smitten of God, and afflicted.

But he was wounded for our transgressions, he was bruised for our iniquities: the chastisement of our peace was upon him; and with his stripes we are healed.

All we like sheep have gone astray; we have turned every one to his own way; and the LORD hath laid on him the iniquity of us all.

He was oppressed, and he was afflicted, yet he opened not his mouth: he is brought as a lamb to the slaughter, and as a sheep before her shearers is dumb, so he openeth not his mouth.

He was taken from prison and from judgment: and who shall declare his generation? for he was cut off out of the land of the living: for the transgression of my people was he stricken.

And he made his grave with the wicked, and with the rich in his death; because he had done no violence, neither was any deceit in his mouth.

Yet it pleased the LORD to bruise him; he hath put him to grief: when thou shalt make his soul an offering for sin, he shall see his seed, he shall prolong his days, and the pleasure of the LORD shall prosper in his hand.

He shall see of the travail of his soul, and shall be satisfied: by his knowledge shall my righteous servant justify many; for he shall bear their iniquities.

Therefore will I divide him a portion with the great, and he shall divide the spoil with the strong; because he hath poured out his soul unto death: and he was numbered with the transgressors; and he bare the sin of many, and made intercession for the transgressors.

(Authorized [King James] Version)

Amazing grace

The first six verses of this hymn were the work of hymn writer John Newton; the last was a later addition by John P. Rees (1825–1900). Newton turned to the church after a dissolute life in which he had even operated as a slave-trader. As curate in the Northamptonshire village of Olney he dedicated himself to God's work, refusing to retire due to ill-health even in his eighties, arguing 'My memory is nearly gone, but I remember two things: that I am a great sinner, and that Christ is a great Saviour!'

This hymn is unique in having occupied the number one spot in the pop charts for a total of nine weeks in a version recorded by the pipes and drums of the Royal Scots Dragoon Guards in the early 1970s.

Amazing grace! how sweet the sound
That saved a wretch like me;
I once was lost, but now am found,
Was blind, but now I see.

'Twas grace that taught my heart to fear,
And grace my fears relieved;
How precious did that grace appear,
The hour I first believed!

Through many dangers, toils and snares
I have already come:
'Tis grace that brought me safe thus far,
And grace will lead me home.

The Lord has promised good to me,
His word my hope secures;
He will my shield and portion be
As long as life endures.

Yes, when this heart and flesh shall fail,
And mortal life shall cease,
I shall possess within the veil
A life of joy and peace.

The earth shall soon dissolve like snow,
The sun forbear to shine,
But God, who called me here below,
Will be for ever mine.

When we've been there a thousand years,
Bright shining as the sun,
We've no less days to sing God's praise
Than when we first begun.

John Newton (1725–1807)

And can it be?

This hymn was among the very first of the 8000 or so hymns written by the great hymn writer Charles Wesley over the course of 50 years. It was probably conceived shortly after 21 May 1738, the day upon which Charles underwent a revelatory conversion to evangelicalism under the influence of the Moravian missionary Peter Boehler. It is also said to have been sung by Charles' brother John on the evening of his own conversion some time later.

And can it be that I should gain
An interest in the Saviour's blood?
Died He for me, who caused His pain?
For me, who Him to death pursued?
Amazing love! how can it be
That Thou, my Lord, shouldst die for me?

He left His Father's throne above,
So free, so infinite His grace!
Emptied Himself of all but love,
And bled for Adam's helpless race!
'Tis mercy all, immense and free,
For, O my God, it found out me.

'Tis mystery all! th' Immortal dies!
Who can explore his strange design?
In vain the firstborn seraph tries
To sound the depths of love divine.
'Tis mercy all! let earth adore;
Let angel minds inquire no more.

Long my imprisoned spirit lay
Fast bound in sin and nature's night.
Thine eye diffused a quickening ray;
I woke – the dungeon flamed with light!
My chains fell off, my heart was free,
I rose, went forth, and followed Thee.

No condemnation now I dread;
Jesus, and all in Him is mine;
Alive in Him, my living Head,
And clothed in righteousness divine,
Bold I approach th' eternal throne,
And claim the crown, through Christ my own.

Charles Wesley (1707–88)

Away in a manger

Extraordinarily, no one knows who wrote this hugely popular children's Christmas carol, although the third verse is known to have been the work of John Thomas McFarland (1851–1913). Because it was first published in a Lutheran hymnal early in the nineteenth century it was assumed for many years that it was composed by Martin Luther himself, but this appears to be an erroneous attribution.

Away in a manger, no crib for a bed,
The little Lord Jesus laid down His sweet head;
The stars in the bright sky looked down where He lay –
The little Lord Jesus, asleep on the hay.

The cattle are lowing, the baby awakes,
But little Lord Jesus, no crying He makes.
I love Thee, Lord Jesus! Look down from the sky,
And stay by my side until morning is nigh.

Be near me, Lord Jesus: I ask Thee to stay
Close by me for ever, and love me, I pray;
Bless all the dear children in Thy tender care,
And fit us for heaven to live with Thee there.

Anonymous

Be baptized

This passage from Acts 2:38–42 contains the best-known call to discipleship from the early church. Peter, who had been fearful and timid, denying Christ three times, has been empowered by the Holy Spirit and is now proclaiming the good news boldly and fearlessly. The results are dramatic as many come to believe in Jesus Christ.

Peter said to them, 'Repent, and be baptized every one of you in the name of Jesus Christ so that your sins may be forgiven; and you will receive the gift of the Holy Spirit. For the promise is for you, for your children, and for all who are far away, everyone whom the LORD our God calls to him.' And he testified with many other arguments and exhorted them, saying, 'Save yourselves from this corrupt generation.' So those who welcomed his message were baptized, and that day about three thousand persons were added. They devoted themselves to the apostles' teaching and fellowship, to the breaking of bread and the prayers.

Be still, my soul

Katharina Amalia von Schlegel was the canoness of a women's seminary in post-Reformation Germany and a leading figure in the Pietist movement. This hymn became a great favourite among English speakers after being translated by Jane Laurie Borthwick (1813–97), a dedicated member of the Free Church of Scotland. It owes much of its success to its setting to Sibelius' music Finlandia.

Be still, my soul: the Lord is on thy side;
Bear patiently the cross of grief or pain;
Leave to thy God to order and provide;
In every change He faithful will remain.
Be still, my soul: thy best, thy heavenly friend
Through thorny ways leads to a joyful end.

Be still, my soul: thy God doth undertake
To guide the future as He has the past.
Thy hope, thy confidence let nothing shake;
All now mysterious shall be bright at last.
Be still, my soul: the waves and winds still know
His voice who ruled them while He dwelt below.

Be still, my soul: when dearest friends depart,
And all is darkened in the vale of tears,
Then shalt thou better know His love, His heart,
Who comes to soothe thy sorrow and thy fears.
Be still, my soul: thy Jesus can repay,
From His own fullness, all He takes away.

Be still, my soul: the hour is hastening on
When we shall be forever with the Lord,
When disappointment, grief, and fear are gone,
Sorrow forgot, love's purest joys restored.
Be still, my soul: when change and tears are past,
All safe and blessed we shall meet at last.

Katharina Amalia von Schlegel (1697–1768)

Be Thou my vision

The words for this hymn come originally from an eighth-century Irish poem entitled 'Rob tu mo bhoile'. It became a great favourite with Irish congregations after first appearing in The Irish Church Hymnal (1919), translated by Mary Elizabeth Byrne (1880–1931) and set to music by Eleanor Henrietta Hull (1860–1935).

Be Thou my vision, O Lord of my heart,
Be all else but naught to me, save that Thou art,
Be Thou my best thought in the day and the night,
Both waking and sleeping, Thy presence my light.

Be Thou my wisdom, be Thou my true word,
Be Thou ever with me, and I with Thee, Lord,
Be Thou my great Father, and I Thy true son,
Be Thou in me dwelling, and I with Thee one.

Be Thou my breastplate, my sword for the fight,
Be Thou my whole armour, be Thou my true might,
Be Thou my soul's shelter, be Thou my strong tower,
O raise Thou me heavenward, great Power of my power.

Riches I heed not, nor man's empty praise,
Be Thou my inheritance now and always,
Be Thou and Thou only the first in my heart,
O Sovereign of heaven, my treasure Thou art.

High King of heaven, Thou heaven's bright Sun,
O grant me its joys after vict'ry is won,
Great heart of my own heart, whatever befall,
Still be Thou my vision, O Ruler of all.

Anonymous

Blessed are the poor in spirit

This passage, from Matthew 5:1–12, is often quoted as comfort for those who are experiencing difficulties in their lives. The eight blessings announced by Christ at the start of the Sermon on the Mount are known as 'The Beatitudes'.

When Jesus saw the crowds, he went up the mountain; and after he sat down, his disciples came to him. Then he began to speak, and taught them, saying:

'Blessed are the poor in spirit, for theirs is the kingdom of heaven.

'Blessed are those who mourn, for they will be comforted.

'Blessed are the meek, for they will inherit the earth.

'Blessed are those who hunger and thirst for righteousness, for they will be filled.

'Blessed are the merciful, for they will receive mercy.

'Blessed are the pure in heart, for they will see God.

'Blessed are the peacemakers, for they will be called children of God.

'Blessed are those who are persecuted for righteousness' sake, for theirs is the kingdom of heaven.

'Blessed are you when people revile you and persecute you and utter all kinds of evil against you falsely on my account. Rejoice and be glad, for your reward is great in heaven, for in the same way they persecuted the prophets who were before you.'

Blessed assurance, Jesus is mine

Fanny Crosby wrote over 8000 hymns, of which this is one of the most celebrated. A native of Putnam County, New York, Fanny was born blind and attended one of the first special schools for the blind in the USA. She overcame her blindness by composing her lines in her head and then dictating them to be written down by a friend or secretary, publishing her vast output under no fewer than 216 pseudonyms.

In the latter part of the twentieth century this particular hymn was adopted as a theme tune by celebrated US evangelist Billy Graham.

Blessed assurance, Jesus is mine!
O what a foretaste of glory divine!
Heir of salvation, purchase of God;
Born of His Spirit, washed in His blood.

This is my story, this is my song,
Praising my Saviour all the day long;
This is my story, this is my song,
Praising my Saviour all the day long.

Perfect submission, perfect delight,
Visions of rapture burst on my sight;
Angels descending, bring from above
Echoes of mercy, whispers of love.

Perfect submission, all is at rest,
I in my Saviour am happy and blest;
Watching and waiting, looking above,
Filled with His goodness, lost in His love.

Fanny Crosby (Frances van Alstyne; 1820–1915)

Blood, toil, tears and sweat

Winston Churchill delivered this speech (his first in the post of British Prime Minister) on 13 May 1940, when the country faced the threat of invasion by Nazi Germany. It remains one of the most celebrated expressions of determination in the face of danger.

I would say to the House, as I said to those who have joined this government: 'I have nothing to offer but blood, toil, tears and sweat.'

We have before us an ordeal of the most grievous kind. We have before us many, many long months of struggle and of suffering.

You ask, what is our policy? I can say: It is to wage war, by sea, land and air, with all our might and with all the strength that God can give us; to wage war against a monstrous tyranny, never surpassed in the dark, lamentable catalogue of human crime. That is our policy.

You ask, what is our aim? I can answer in one word: It is victory, victory at all costs, victory in spite of all terror, victory, however long and hard the road may be; for without victory, there is no survival.

Let that be realised; no survival for the British Empire, no survival for all that the British Empire has stood for, no survival for the urge and impulse of the ages, that mankind will move forward towards its goal. But I take up my task with buoyancy and hope.

I feel sure that our cause will not be suffered to fail among men. At this time I feel entitled to claim the aid of all, and I say, 'Come then, let us go forward together with our united strength.'

Winston Churchill (1874–1965)

Breathe on me, Breath of God

This hymn was first published in 1878 and remains popular today. It links the breath of God with the Holy Spirit whose person and activity are vital at every stage of the Christian life, from new birth and yearning for purity and a Christ-like life, through to eternal life.

Breathe on me, Breath of God,
Fill me with life anew,
That I may love what Thou dost love,
And do what Thou wouldst do.

Breathe on me, Breath of God,
Until my heart is pure;
Until with Thee I will one will,
To do and to endure.

Breathe on me, Breath of God,
Till I am wholly Thine;
Until this earthly part of me
Glows with Thy fire divine.

Breathe on me, Breath of God:
So shall I never die,
But live with Thee the perfect life
Of Thine eternity.

Edwin Hatch (1835–89)

The burning bush

The story of the Burning Bush, as described at Exodus 3:1–14, ranks among the best-known episodes in the Old Testament. It is much cherished by those who seek evidence of God's commitment to those who are suffering or in need of guidance.

Moses was keeping the flock of his father-in-law Jethro, the priest of Midian; he led his flock beyond the wilderness, and came to Horeb, the mountain of God. There the angel of the LORD appeared to him in a flame of fire out of a bush; he looked, and the bush was blazing, yet it was not consumed. Then Moses said, 'I must turn aside and look at this great sight, and see why the bush is not burned up.' When the LORD saw that he had turned aside to see, God called to him out of the bush, 'Moses, Moses!' And he said, 'Here I am.' Then he said, 'Come no closer! Remove the sandals from your feet, for the place on which you are standing is holy ground.' He said further, 'I am the God of your father, the God of Abraham, the God of Isaac, and the God of Jacob.' And Moses hid his face, for he was afraid to look at God.

Then the LORD said, 'I have observed the misery of my people who are in Egypt; I have heard their cry on account of their taskmasters. Indeed, I know their sufferings, and I have come down to deliver them from the Egyptians, and to bring them up out of that land to a good and broad land, a land flowing with milk and honey, to the country of the Canaanites, the Hittites, the Amorites, the Perizzites, the Hivites, and the Jebusites. The cry of the Israelites has now come to me; I have also seen how the Egyptians oppress them. So come, I will send you to Pharaoh to bring my people, the Israelites, out of Egypt.' But Moses said to God, 'Who am I that I should go to Pharaoh, and bring the Israelites out of Egypt?' He said, 'I will be with you; and this shall be the sign for you that it is I who sent you: when you have brought the people out of Egypt, you shall worship God on this mountain.'

But Moses said to God, 'If I come to the Israelites and say to them, "The God of your ancestors has sent me to you," and they ask me, "What is his name?" what shall I say to them?'

God said to Moses, 'I AM WHO I AM.' He said further, 'Thus you shall say to the Israelites, "I AM has sent me to you."'

Christ, the Lord, is risen today

This triumphant hymn is among the most popular penned by Charles Wesley, author of over 8000 hymns. It is often sung at Easter, but may also be heard in churches at other times of the year.

Christ the Lord is risen today, Alleluia!
Sons of men and angels say, Alleluia!
Raise your joys and triumphs high, Alleluia!
Sing, ye heavens, and earth reply, Alleluia!

Lives again our glorious king, Alleluia!
Where, O death, is now thy sting? Alleluia!
Once He died, our souls to save, Alleluia!
Where's thy victory, boasting grave? Alleluia!

Love's redeeming work is done, Alleluia!
Fought the fight, the battle won, Alleluia!
Death in vain forbids Him rise, Alleluia!
Christ hath opened paradise, Alleluia!

Soar we now where Christ has led, Alleluia!
Following our exalted Head, Alleluia!
Made like Him, like Him we rise, Alleluia!
Ours the cross, the grave, the skies, Alleluia!

Charles Wesley (1707–88)

Christ triumphant

This hymn, first published in 1966, has proved to be a popular addition to hymn books. It summarises the nature and characteristics of Jesus Christ, making reference to His birth, His death on the cross and His resurrection. It has become a popular choice for Easter Day services.

Christ triumphant, ever reigning,
Saviour, Master, King.
Lord of heaven, our lives sustaining,
Hear us as we sing:
Yours the glory and the crown,
The high renown, the eternal name.

Word incarnate, truth revealing,
Son of Man on earth!
Power and majesty concealing
By your humble birth:
Yours the glory and the crown,
The high renown, the eternal name.

Suffering servant, scorned, ill-treated,
Victim crucified!
Death is through the cross defeated,
Sinners justified:
Yours the glory and the crown,
The high renown, the eternal name.

Priestly king, enthroned for ever
High in heaven above!
Sin and death and hell shall never
Stifle hymns of love:
Yours the glory and thc crown,
The high renown, the eternal name.

So, our hearts and voices raising
Through the ages long,
Ceaselessly upon you gazing,
This shall be our song:
Yours the glory and the crown,
The high renown, the eternal name.

Michael Saward (b.1932)

The Church's one foundation

This hymn was the work of a curate at Windsor who intended it as a tribute to his contemporary Bishop Gray of Capetown. Gray had attracted Stone's admiration after speaking out against the liberal Bishop Colenso of Natal, who stood accused of questioning the church's traditional stand on a number of issues – hence the reference to schisms in the third verse. The original hymn included an extra verse (long since dropped) that included the lines 'Though there be those who hate her / And false sons in her pale / Against or foe or traitor / She ever shall prevail.'

The Church's one foundation
Is Jesus Christ, her Lord;
She is His new creation
By water and the word:
From heaven He came and sought her
To be His holy bride;
With His own blood He bought her,
And for her life He died.

Elect from every nation,
Yet one o'er all the earth,
Her charter of salvation
One Lord, one faith, one birth:
One holy name she blesses,
Partakes one holy food,
And to one hope she presses
With every grace endued.

Though with a scornful wonder
Men see her sore oppressed,
By schisms rent asunder,
By heresies distressed;
Yet saints their watch are keeping,
Their cry goes up, 'How long?'
And soon the night of weeping
Shall be the morn of song.

'Mid toil and tribulation,
And tumult of her war,
She waits the consummation
Of peace for evermore;
Till with the vision glorious
Her longing eyes are blest,
And the great Church victorious
Shall be the Church at rest.

Yet she on earth hath union
With God the Three in One,
And mystic sweet communion
With those whose rest is won:
O happy ones and holy!
Lord, give us grace that we
Like them, the meek and lowly,
On high may dwell with Thee.

Samuel John Stone (1839–1900)

Come, ye thankful people, come

The work of the noted scholar Dean Henry Alford of Canterbury, 'Come, ye thankful people, come' is an established favourite with congregations at harvest festivals, although it appears in a number of variant forms. Its original title was, indeed, 'After Harvest'. Alford had had a precocious start as a hymn writer, publishing a Collection of Hymns for Sundry Occasions at the tender age of 11.

Come, ye thankful people, come,
Raise the song of harvest-home!
All be safely gathered in,
Ere the winter storms begin;
God, our Maker, doth provide
For our wants to be supplied;
Come to God's own temple, come,
Raise the song of harvest-home!

All the world is God's own field,
Fruit unto his praise to yield,
Wheat and tares together sown,
Unto joy or sorrow grown:
First the blade and then the ear,
Then the full corn shall appear:
Grant, O harvest Lord, that we
Wholesome grain and pure may be.

For the Lord our God shall come,
And shall take his harvest home;
From his field shall purge away
All that doth offend, that day;
Give his angels charge at last
In the fire the tares to cast,
But the fruitful ears to store
In his garner evermore.

Even so, Lord, quickly come;
Bring thy final harvest home;
Gather thou thy people in,
Free from sorrow, free from sin,
There for ever purified
In thy garner to abide:
Come, with all thine angels come,
Raise the glorious harvest-home!

Henry Alford (1810–71)

Come down, O love divine

This hymn was written by the Italian Bianco da Siena. He trained originally as an apprentice in wool in Siena and at 17 became a member of a mystic lay order that followed St Augustine's rule. He was the author of several hymns. This particular hymn, a favourite choice for weddings, asks the Holy Spirit to fill the hearts of the faithful with a deep sense of God's presence. It owes its modern popularity to the tune ('Down Ampney') composed for this hymn by the English composer Ralph Vaughan Williams.

Come down, O love divine,
Seek Thou this soul of mine,
And visit it with Thine own ardour glowing.
O comforter, draw near,
Within my heart appear,
And kindle it, Thy holy flame bestowing.

O let it freely burn,
Till earthly passions turn
To dust and ashes in its heat consuming;
And let Thy glorious light
Shine ever on my sight,
And clothe me round, the while my path illuming.

Let holy charity
Mine outward vesture be,
And lowliness become mine inner clothing;
True lowliness of heart,
Which takes the humbler part,
And o'er its own shortcomings weeps with loathing.

And so the yearning strong,
With which the soul will long,
Shall far outpass the power of human telling;
For none can guess its grace,
Till he become the place
Wherein the Holy Spirit makes His dwelling.

Bianco da Siena (c.1350–1434)

Come live with me and be my love

Christopher Marlowe was first and foremost a playwright, the first great dramatist of the Elizabethan era and a major influence on the early work of William Shakespeare. This sensuous poem in praise of love, first published in 1599, is something of an oddity in his output. He appears to have written no other short poems and what we know of his life is completely at odds with the peaceable pastoral scene evoked here – though Marlowe's subject must have been better off than the average shepherd to be able to offer his love golden buckles and silver dishes.

Come live with me and be my love,
And we will all the pleasures prove
That valleys, groves, hills, and fields,
Woods, or steepy mountain yields.

And we will sit upon the rocks,
Seeing shepherds feed their flocks,
By shallow rivers to whose falls
Melodious birds sing madrigals.

And I will make thee beds of roses
And a thousand fragrant posies,
A cap of flowers, and a kirtle
Embroidered all with leaves of myrtle.

A gown made of the finest wool,
Which from our pretty lambs we pull,
Fair lined slippers for the cold:
With buckles of the purest gold.

A belt of straw, and ivy buds,
With coral clasps and amber studs,
And if these pleasures may thee move,
Come live with me, and be my love.

The shepherd's swains shall dance and sing,
For thy delight each May-morning,
If these delights thy mind may move;
Then live with me, and be my love.

Christopher Marlowe (1564–93)

Crossing the bar

This consolatory poem is often recited at funerals to assuage the grief of mourners. The allusion in the title is to a vessel passing over an offshore ridge of sand, mud or shingle marking the entrance to a harbour or river, used here as an allegory for the departure of the soul at death.

Sunset and evening star,
And one clear call for me!
And may there be no moaning of the bar,
When I put out to sea.

But such a tide as moving seems asleep,
Too full for sound and foam,
When that which drew from out the boundless deep
Turns again home.

Twilight and evening bell,
And after that the dark!
And may there be no sadness of farewell,
When I embark;

For tho' from out our bourne of Time and Place
The flood may bear me far,
I hope to see my Pilot face to face
When I have crost the bar.

Alfred, Lord Tennyson (1809–92)

Crown Him with many crowns

In its original form this hymn, initially entitled 'The Song of the Seraphs', was the work of Matthew Bridges, who became a Roman Catholic at the age of 48. Some 30 years later, however, an Anglican clergyman named Godfrey Thring felt the need to add new lines referring specifically to the resurrection and, with Bridges' blessing (although it seems the two men never actually met), added a new verse describing Christ's triumph over death. Like many other hymns, this appears in a number of variant forms, sometimes including alterations made subsequently by Percy Dearmer (1867–1936).

Crown Him with many crowns,
The lamb upon His throne;
Hark! how the heavenly anthem drowns
All music but its own:
Awake, my soul, and sing
Of Him who died for thee,
And hail Him as thy matchless king
Through all eternity.

Crown Him the Son of God
Before the worlds began;
And ye who tread where He hath trod,
Crown Him the Son of Man,
Who every grief hath known
That wrings the human breast,
And takes and bears them for His own,
That all in Him may rest.

Crown Him the Lord of love,
Behold His hands and side,
Those wounds yet visible above
In beauty glorified:
No angel in the sky
Can fully bear that sight,
But downward bends his burning eye
At mysteries so bright.

Crown Him the Lord of life,
Who triumphed o'er the grave,
And rose victorious in the strife
For those He came to save:
His glories now we sing
Who died, and rose on high;
Who died eternal life to bring,
And lives that death may die.

Crown Him the Lord of peace,
Whose power a sceptre sways
From pole to pole, that wars may cease,
And all be prayer and praise:
His reign shall know no end,
And round His pierced feet
Fair flowers of paradise extend
Their fragrance ever sweet.

Crown Him the Lord of years,
The Potentate of time,
Creator of the rolling spheres,
Ineffably sublime:
All hail, Redeemer, hail!
For Thou hast died for me:
Thy praise shall never, never fail
Throughout eternity.
Matthew Bridges (1800–94) and Godfrey Thring (1823–1903)

Daniel in the lions' den

The story of Daniel, recounted at Daniel 6:19–28, has long been cherished as an example of God's protective love, providing encouragement and comfort for those facing considerable danger or difficulty in their lives.

Then, at break of day, the king got up and hurried to the den of lions. When he came near the den where Daniel was, he cried out anxiously to Daniel, 'O Daniel, servant of the living God, has your God whom you faithfully serve been able to deliver you from the lions?' Daniel then said to the king, 'O king, live for ever! My God sent his angel and shut the lions' mouths so that they would not hurt me, because I was found blameless before him; and also before you, O king, I have done no wrong.' Then the king was exceedingly glad and commanded that Daniel be taken up out of the den. So Daniel was taken up out of the den, and no kind of harm was found on him, because he had trusted in his God. The king gave a command, and those who had accused Daniel were brought and thrown into the den of lions – they, their children, and their wives. Before they reached the bottom of the den the lions overpowered them and broke all their bones in pieces.

Then King Darius wrote to all peoples and nations of every language throughout the whole world: 'May you have abundant prosperity! I make a decree, that in all my royal dominion people should tremble and fear before the God of Daniel: For he is the living God, enduring for ever. His kingdom shall never be destroyed, and his dominion has no end. He delivers and rescues, he works signs and wonders in heaven and on earth; for he has saved Daniel from the power of the lions.' So this Daniel prospered during the reign of Darius and the reign of Cyrus the Persian.

David and Goliath

The story of David and Goliath, as given at 1 Samuel 17:38–51, represents the archetype of the underdog triumphing against seemingly overwhelming opposition. It remains a reassuring reminder that what appears impossible may yet prove attainable to the heart that has faith in God.

Saul clothed David with his armour; he put a bronze helmet on his head and clothed him with a coat of mail. David strapped Saul's sword over the armour, and he tried in vain to walk, for he was not used to them. Then David said to Saul, 'I cannot walk with these; for I am not used to them.' So David removed them. Then he took his staff in his hand, and chose five smooth stones from the wadi, and put them in his shepherd's bag, in the pouch; his sling was in his hand, and he drew near to the Philistine.

The Philistine came on and drew near to David, with his shield-bearer in front of him. When the Philistine looked and saw David, he disdained him, for he was only a youth, ruddy and handsome in appearance. The Philistine said to David, 'Am I a dog, that you come to me with sticks?' And the Philistine cursed David by his gods. The Philistine said to David, 'Come to me, and I will give your flesh to the birds of the air and to the wild animals of the field.' But David said to the Philistine, 'You come to me with sword and spear and javelin; but I come to you in the name of the LORD of hosts, the God of the armies of Israel, whom you have defied. This very day the LORD will deliver you into my hand, and I will strike you down and cut off your head; and I will give the dead bodies of the Philistine army this very day to the birds of the air and to the wild animals of the earth, so that all the earth may know that there is a God in Israel, and that all this assembly may know that the LORD does not save by sword and spear; for the battle is the LORD's and he will give you into our hand.'

When the Philistine drew nearer to meet David, David ran quickly towards the battle line to meet the Philistine. David put his hand in his bag, took out a stone, slung it, and struck the Philistine on his forehead; the stone sank into his forehead, and he fell face down on the ground.

So David prevailed over the Philistine with a sling and a stone, striking down the Philistine and killing him; there was no sword in David's hand. Then David ran and stood over the Philistine; he grasped his sword, drew it out of its sheath, and killed him; then he cut off his head with it.

When the Philistines saw that their champion was dead, they fled.

The day Thou gavest, Lord, is ended

This popular evening hymn was written by the Victorian clergyman and hymn writer John Ellerton, who was rector at Barnes and subsequently Torquay. It brought its author considerable posthumous prestige when it was chosen (largely because of its imperial overtones) by Queen Victoria to be sung at her Diamond Jubilee service in St Paul's Cathedral in 1897.

The day Thou gavest, Lord, is ended,
The darkness falls at Thy behest;
To Thee our morning hymns ascended,
Thy praise shall sanctify our rest.

We thank Thee that Thy Church unsleeping,
While earth rolls onward into light,
Through all the world her watch is keeping,
And rests not now by day or night.

As o'er each continent and island
The dawn leads on another day,
The voice of prayer is never silent,
Nor dies the strain of praise away.

The sun that bids us rest is waking
Our brethren 'neath the western sky,
And hour by hour fresh lips are making
Thy wondrous doings heard on high.

So be it, Lord; Thy throne shall never,
Like earth's proud empires, pass away;
Thy kingdom stands and grows for ever,
Till all Thy creatures own Thy sway.

John Ellerton (1826–93)

Dear Lord and Father of mankind

John Greenleaf Whittier never intended these verses from the larger poetic work The Brewing of Soma *(1872) to be sung as, being a committed Quaker, he did not approve of the use of music in public worship. The son of a farmer, he considered himself a poet rather than a hymn writer but after his words were matched with Sir Hubert Parry's tune 'Repton' from the oratorio Judith (1888) they became a popular choice with congregations of many different kinds. The 'soma' referred to in the title of Whittier's work was an intoxicating drink used by a Hindu sect in India to drive themselves into an ecstatic frenzy far removed from the poet's 'still small voice of calm'.*

Dear Lord and Father of mankind,
Forgive our foolish ways!
Reclothe us in our rightful mind;
In purer lives Thy service find,
In deeper reverence, praise.

In simple trust like theirs who heard
Beside the Syrian sea
The gracious calling of the Lord,
Let us, like them, without a word,
Rise up and follow Thee.

O Sabbath rest by Galilee!
O calm of hills above,
Where Jesus knelt to share with Thee
The silence of eternity
Interpreted by love!

With that deep hush subduing all
Our words and works that drown
The tender whisper of Thy call,
As noiseless let Thy blessing fall
As fell Thy manna down.

Drop Thy still dews of quietness,
Till all our strivings cease;
Take from our souls the strain and stress,
And let out ordered lives confess
The beauty of Thy peace.

Breathe through the heats of our desire
Thy coolness and Thy balm;
Let sense be dumb, let flesh retire;
Speak through the earthquake, wind, and fire,
O still small voice of calm!

John Greenleaf Whittier (1807–92)

Death, be not proud

John Donne's 'Death, be not Proud' ranks among the most familiar of his Holy Sonnets *probably written around 1610–11. It is often quoted at funerals as a refutation of death's triumph over life. Donne himself had no doubt about the certainty of his own eventual resurrection, even having himself painted wearing a shroud and standing upon a funeral urn as he might appear at the Last Judgement.*

Death, be not proud, though some have callèd thee
Mighty and dreadful, for thou art not so:
For those whom thou think'st thou dost overthrow
Die not, poor Death; nor yet canst thou kill me.
From Rest and Sleep, which but thy pictures be,
Much pleasure, then, from thee much more must flow;
And soonest our best men with thee do go –
Rest of their bones and souls' delivery.
Thou'rt slave to fate, chance, kings, and desperate men,
And dost with poison, war, and sickness dwell;
And poppy or charms can make us sleep as well
And better than thy stroke. Why swell'st thou then?
One short sleep past, we wake eternally,
And Death shall be no more: Death, thou shalt die.

John Donne (c.1572–1631)

Death is nothing at all

Henry Scott Holland was an English clergyman who served as Canon of St Paul's Cathedral in the years 1884–1911. Although he also published sermons, various books on faith and a biography of Swedish soprano Jenny Lind, it is for this simple message of comfort to the bereaved that he is usually remembered. It is sometimes encountered in slightly altered form to include the lines 'Let my name be ever the household word that it always was, Let it be spoken without an effort, Without the ghost of a shadow upon it.'

Death is nothing at all,
I have only slipped away into the next room.
I am I, and you are you,
Whatever we were to each other, that we still are.
Call me by my old familiar name,
Speak to me in the easy way which you always used.
Put no difference in your tone,
Wear no forced air of solemnity or sorrow
Laugh as we always laughed at the little jokes we enjoyed
together.
Let my name be ever the household word that it always was,
Let it be spoken without effect,
Without the trace of a shadow on it.
Life means all that it ever meant
It is the same as it ever was.
There is unbroken continuity.
Why should I be out of mind because I am out of sight?
I am waiting for you,
For an interval,
Somewhere very near,
Just around the corner
All is Well.

Henry Scott Holland (1847–1918)

Do not go gentle into that good night

This fierce protest by Welsh poet Dylan Thomas against placid acceptance of death is often quoted as a spur to those who surrender themselves to complacency and resignation. Thomas himself famously drank himself to death, leaving the world as passionately and recklessly as he had lived.

Do not go gentle into that good night,
Old age should burn and rave at close of day;
Rage, rage against the dying of the light.

Though wise men at their end know dark is right,
Because their words had forked no lightning they
Do not go gentle into that good night.

Good men, the last wave by, crying how bright
Their frail deeds might have danced in a green bay,
Rage, rage against the dying of the light.

Wild men who caught and sang the sun in flight,
And learn, too late, they grieved it on its way,
Do not go gentle into that good night.

Grave men, near death, who see with blinding sight
Blind eyes could blaze like meteors and be gay,
Rage, rage against the dying of the light.

And you, my father, there on the sad height,
Curse, bless, me now with your fierce tears, I pray.
Do not go gentle into that good night.
Rage, rage against the dying of the light.

Dylan Thomas (1914–53)

Do not stand at my grave and weep

Authorship of the following piece, which has become a favourite consolatory reading at funeral services, has been disputed and it has been variously identified as a Native American funeral prayer or an item from a Victorian magazine. It would appear, however, to have been written in 1932 by the US poet Mary Elizabeth Frye. It became more widely known in the latter part of the twentieth century through its exposure after a copy of it, addressed to his parents, was found in the pocket of Steven Cummins, a British soldier killed on active service in Northern Ireland.

Do not stand at my grave and weep;
I am not there. I do not sleep.
I am a thousand winds that blow.
I am the diamond glints on snow.
I am the sunlight on ripened grain.
I am the gentle autumn rain.
When you awaken in the morning's hush
I am the swift uplifting rush
Of quiet birds in circling flight.
I am the soft stars that shine at night.
Do not stand at my grave and cry;
I am not there. I did not die.

Mary Elizabeth Frye (b.1904)

Do not worry

Matthew 6:25–34 ranks among the most highly regarded passages from the Bible when judged as literature. A reminder to all the faithful to abandon worldly concerns and to trust themselves instead to God's bounty, it offers substantial consolation to those who are disillusioned or disappointed in their hopes of material gain.

Therefore I tell you, do not worry about your life, what you will eat or what you will drink, or about your body, what you will wear. Is not life more than food, and the body more than clothing? Look at the birds of the air; they neither sow nor reap nor gather into barns, and yet your heavenly Father feeds them. Are you not of more value than they? And can any of you by worrying add a single hour to your span of life? And why do you worry about clothing? Consider the lilies of the field, how they grow; they neither toil nor spin, Yet I tell you, even Solomon in all his glory was not clothed like one of these. But if God so clothes the grass of the field, which is alive today and tomorrow is thrown into the oven, will he not much more clothe you – you of little faith? Therefore do not worry, saying 'What will we eat?' or 'What will we drink?' or 'What will we wear?' For it is the Gentiles who strive for all these things; and indeed your heavenly Father knows that you need all these things. But strive first for the kingdom of God and his righteousness, and all these things will be given to you as well.

So do not worry about tomorrow, for tomorrow will bring worries of its own. Today's trouble is enough for today.

Drink to me only with thine eyes

This love poem by Ben Jonson was first published in the miscellany entitled The Forest *(1616). Today it is a popular choice of reading at wedding celebrations.*

Drink to me only with thine eyes,
And I will pledge with mine;
Or leave a kiss but in the cup
And I'll not look for wine.
The thirst that from the soul doth rise
Doth ask a drink divine;
But might I of Jove's nectar sup,
I would not change for thine.

I sent thee late a rosy wreath,
Not so much honouring thee
As giving it a hope that there
It could not wither'd be;
But thou thereon didst only breathe
And sent'st it back to me;
Since when it grows, and smells, I swear,
Not of itself but thee!

Ben Jonson (1572–1637)

Each eve Earth falleth down the dark

This poem by the English poet, artist and designer William Morris celebrates the revival of life and hope through faith and has a clear religious message. It remains a poignant source of consolation and encouragement to those who face disappointment or disillusionment.

Each eve Earth falleth down the dark,
As though its hopes were o'er;
Yet lurks the sun when day is done
Behind tomorrow's door.

Grey grows the dawn while men-folk sleep,
Unseen spreads on the light,
Till the thrush sings to the coloured things,
And earth forgets her night.

No otherwise wends on our Hope;
E'en as a tale that's told
Are fair lives lost, and all the cost
Of wise and true and bold.

We've toiled and failed; we spake the word;
None hearkened; dumb we lie;
Our Hope is dead, the seed we spread
Fell o'er the Earth to die.

What's this? For joy our hearts stand still,
And life is loved and dear,
The lost and found the Cause hath crowned,
The Day of Days is here.

William Morris (1834–96)

Eternal Father, strong to save

This evergreen hymn, published in 1861, is indelibly associated with seafarers and is sometimes called the 'sailors hymn'. Although an unsubstantiated tradition claims that William Whiting, a London-born grocer's son who became Master of the Winchester choirboys, wrote this hymn for one of his choristers who was about to leave for America, it seems Whiting rather intended his lines to be interpreted as a metaphor for baptism and the 'restless wave' to stand for the world and all its troubles. The tune, written by John Bacchus Dykes, is called 'Melita', this being a reference to Malta (the place where St Paul was shipwrecked, according to Acts 27).

Eternal Father, strong to save,
Whose arm doth bind the restless wave,
Who bidd'st the mighty ocean deep
Its own appointed limits keep;
O hear us when we cry to Thee
For those in peril on the sea.

O Saviour, whose almighty word
The winds and waves submissive heard,
Who walkedst on the foaming deep,
And calm amid its rage didst sleep:
O hear us when we cry to Thee
For those in peril on the sea.

O sacred Spirit, who didst brood
Upon the chaos dark and rude,
Who bad'st its angry tumult cease,
And gavest light and life and peace:
O hear us when we cry to Thee
For those in peril on the sea.

O Trinity of love and power,
Our brethren shield in danger's hour;
From rock and tempest, fire and foe,
Protect them wheresoe'er they go:
And ever let there rise to Thee
Glad hymns of praise from land and sea.

William Whiting (1825–78)

Faith, hope, and love

This biblical passage, from 1 Corinthians 13:1–13, is a favourite choice of reading for marriage services, but it may also be recited on other occasions and remains one of the most oft-repeated descriptions of the generous nature of love. The Authorized (King James) Version of the passage renders 'love' as 'charity'.

If I speak in the tongues of mortals and of angels, but do not have love, I am a noisy gong or a clanging cymbal. And if I have prophetic powers, and understand all mysteries and all knowledge, and if I have all faith, so as to remove mountains, but do not have love, I am nothing. If I give away all my possessions, and if I hand over my body so that I may boast, but do not have love, I gain nothing.

Love is patient; love is kind; love is not envious or boastful or arrogant or rude. It does not insist on its own way; it is not irritable or resentful; it does not rejoice in wrongdoing, but rejoices in the truth. It bears all things, believes all things, hopes all things, endures all things.

Love never ends. But as for prophecies, they will come to an end; as for tongues, they will cease; as for knowledge, it will come to an end. For we know only in part, and we prophesy only in part; but when the complete comes, the partial will come to an end. When I was a child, I spoke like a child, I thought like a child, I reasoned like a child; when I became an adult, I put an end to childish ways. For now we see in a mirror, dimly, but then we will see face to face. Now I know only in part; then I will know fully, even as I have been fully known. And now faith, hope, and love abide, these three; and the greatest of these is love.

Far above rubies

This biblical passage, found at Proverbs 31:1–20, celebrates the virtues of the ideal wife. It is consequently often quoted at wedding celebrations.

The words of King Lemuel. An oracle that his mother taught him:

No, my son! No, son of my womb! No, son of my vows!
Do not give your strength to women, your ways to those who destroy kings.
It is not for kings, O Lemuel, it is not for kings to drink wine, or for rulers to desire strong drink;
or else they will drink and forget what has been decreed, and will pervert the rights of all the afflicted.
Give strong drink to one who is perishing, and wine to those in bitter distress;
let them drink and forget their poverty, and remember their misery no more.
Speak out for those who cannot speak, for the rights of all the destitute.
Speak out, judge righteously, defend the rights of the poor and needy.
A capable wife who can find? She is far more precious than jewels.
The heart of her husband trusts in her, and he will have no lack of gain.
She does him good, and not harm, all the days of her life.
She seeks wool and flax, and works with willing hands.
She is like the ships of the merchant, she brings her food from far away.
She rises while it is still night and provides food for her household and tasks for her servant-girls.
She considers a field and buys it; with the fruit of her hands she plants a vineyard.
She girds herself with strength, and makes her arms strong.
She perceives that her merchandise is profitable. Her lamp does not go out at night.
She puts her hands to the distaff, and her hands hold the spindle.
She opens her hand to the poor, and reaches out her hands to the needy.

(New Revised Standard Version)

Father, hear the prayer we offer

Love Maria Willis was a doctor's wife of Rochester, New York. Though a popular choice of hymn, the rendering of Psalm 23 in this hymn has raised some eyebrows over the years with its apparent contempt for the 'green pastures' and 'still waters' of the biblical source. In reality, the original psalm does not recommend the quiet life over one of righteous struggle.

Father, hear the prayer we offer;
Not for ease that prayer shall be,
But for strength that we may ever
Live our lives courageously.

Not for ever in green pastures
Do we ask our way to be;
But the steep and rugged pathway
May we tread rejoicingly.

Not for ever by still waters
Would we idly rest and stay;
But would smite the living fountains
From the rocks along our way.

Be our strength in hours of weakness,
In our wanderings be our guide;
Through endeavour, failure, danger,
Father, be Thou at our side.

Love Maria Willis (1824–1908)

A father's advice to his son

Sir Henry Sidney served two terms as Lord Deputy of Ireland but is usually remembered today as the father of the celebrated soldier-poet Sir Philip Sidney. His parental advice, offered in a letter to his son while he was at school in Shrewsbury in 1556, has been much repeated over the centuries.

Son Philip,

I have received two letters from you, one written in Latin, the other in French: which I take in good part, and will you to exercise that practice of learning often; for that will stand you in most stead in that profession of life that you are born to live in. And now, since this is my first letter that I ever did write to you, I will not that it be all empty of some advice which my natural care of you provoketh me to wish you to follow, as documents to you in this your tender age.

Let your first action be the lifting up of your mind to Almighty God by hearty prayer; and feelingly digest the words you speak in prayer, with continual meditation and thinking of Him to whom you pray, and of the matter for which you pray. And use this as an ordinary act, and at an ordinary hour; whereby the time itself shall put you in remembrance to do that you are accustomed to do in that time.

Apply your study to such hours as your discreet master doth assign you earnestly... And mark the sense and the matter of that you do read as well as the words; so shall you both enrich your tongue with words and your wit with matter, and judgment will grow as years grow in you. Be humble and obedient to your masters, for, unless you frame yourself to obey others – yea, and feel in yourself what obedience is, you shall never be able to teach others to obey you. Be courteous of gesture and affable to all men, with diversity of reverence according to the dignity of the person; there is nothing that winneth so much with so little cost.

Use moderate diet so as, after your meal, you may find your wit fresher, and not duller, and your body lively and not more heavy. Seldom drink wine, and yet sometimes do, lest, being enforced to drink upon the sudden you should not find yourself enflamed. Use exercise of body; yet such as is without peril to your bones or joints.

Above all things tell no untruth; no, not in trifles. The custom of it is naughty... For there cannot be a greater reproach to a gentleman than to be accounted a liar. Study and endeavour yourself to be virtuously occupied. So shall you make such a habit of well-doing in you as you shall not know how to do evil, though you would.

Your Loving father, so long as you fear God.

Sir Henry Sidney (1529–86)

Fight the good fight

The work of John Monsell, Rector of St Nicholas in Guildford, this hymn has remained one of the most popular rallying cries of the Christian church, particularly associated with the Salvation Army. Monsell himself literally gave his life in the service of his calling, dying in an accident while inspecting repairs to the roof of his church. He was a great believer in providing rousing tunes for public worship and criticized the reserve of much church music. His other hymns include 'O worship the Lord in the beauty of holiness'.

Fight the good fight with all thy might!
Christ is thy strength and Christ thy right;
Lay hold on life, and it shall be
Thy joy and crown eternally.

Run the straight race through God's good grace,
Lift up thine eyes, and seek His face;
Life with its way before us lies;
Christ is the path, and Christ the prize.

Cast care aside, lean on thy guide;
His boundless mercy will provide;
Trust, and thy trusting soul shall prove
Christ is its life, and Christ its love.

Faint not nor fear, His arms are near;
He changeth not, and thou art dear;
Only believe, and thou shalt see
That Christ is all in all to thee.

John Samuel Bewley Monsell (1811–75)

For all the saints

A popular choice for All Hallows, but also heard at other times throughout the year, this hymn was the work of William Walsham How, Bishop of East London and later of Wakefield. How was particularly renowned for not resting from his labours, working hard for his parishioners in London's East End and being nicknamed the 'Omnibus Bishop' because he travelled everywhere by bus. The hymn is sung to Ralph Vaughan Williams' 'Sine Nomine'.

For all the saints who from their labours rest,
Who Thee by faith before the world confessed,
Thy name, O Jesu, be for ever blest.
Alleluia! Alleluia!

Thou wast their rock, their fortress, and their might,
Thou, Lord, their Captain in the well-fought fight;
Thou in the darkness drear their one true light.
Alleluia! Alleluia!

O may Thy soldiers, faithful, true, and bold,
Fight as the saints who nobly fought of old,
And win, with them, the victor's crown of gold.
Alleluia! Alleluia!

O blest communion! Fellowship divine!
We feebly struggle, they in glory shine;
Yet all are one in Thee, for all are Thine.
Alleluia! Alleluia!

And when the strife is fierce, the warfare long,
Steals on the ear the distant triumph-song,
And hearts are brave again, and arms are strong.
Alleluia! Alleluia!

The golden evening brightens in the west;
Soon, soon to faithful warriors cometh rest:
Sweet is the calm of paradise the blest.
Alleluia! Alleluia!

But lo! there breaks a yet more glorious day;
The saints triumphant rise in bright array:
The King of glory passes on His way.
Alleluia! Alleluia!

From earth's wide bounds, from ocean's farthest coast,
Through gates of pearl streams in the countless host,
Singing to Father, Son and Holy Ghost.
Alleluia! Alleluia!

William Walsham How (1823–97)

For everything there is a season

This passage, from Ecclesiastes 3:1–8, expresses the belief that things should be allowed to happen at their proper time, according to God's providence. It is sometimes recited at funerals.

For everything there is a season, and a time for every matter under heaven:

a time to be born, and a time to die;
  a time to plant, and a time to pluck up what is planted;
a time to kill, and a time to heal;
  a time to break down, and a time to build up;
a time to weep, and a time to laugh;
  a time to mourn, and a time to dance;
a time to throw away stones, and a time to gather stones together;
  a time to embrace, and a time to refrain from embracing;
a time to seek, and a time to lose;
  a time to keep, and a time to throw away;
a time to tear, and a time to sew;
  a time to keep silence, and a time to speak;
a time to love, and a time to hate;
  a time for war, and a time for peace.

For I dipt into the future

Poet Laureate Alfred, Lord Tennyson's premonitory view of the future of the world in these lines from the longer work 'Locksley Hall' (1842) has impressed many with its accuracy. The idealistic conclusion, however, has made it a favourite of those hoping for a happy ultimate resolution to the world's troubles. Its admirers have included US President Harry Truman, who carried a copy of it in his wallet for some 50 years.

For I dipt into the future, far as human eye could see,
Saw the vision of the world and all the wonder that would be;

Saw the heavens fill with commerce, argosies of magic sails,
Pilots of the purple twilight, dropping down with costly bales;

Heard the heavens fill with shouting, and there rained a
    ghastly dew
From the nations' airy navies grappling in the central blue;

Far along the world-wide whisper of the south wind rushing
    warm,
With the standards of the peoples plunging through the
    thunderstorm;

Till the war drum throbbed no longer, and the battle flags
    were furled
In the Parliament of Man, the Federation of the World.

There the common sense of most shall hold a fretful realm in
    awe,
And the kindly Earth shall slumber, lapt in universal law.

Alfred, Lord Tennyson (1809–92)

For the beauty of the earth

Folliott Sandford Pierpoint is supposed to have been inspired to write this hymn by the view to be seen from a hillside near Bath, where he spent his childhood. An ordained teacher of classics in Cambridge, he intended this hymn to be sung at the offertory of the bread and wine but it has, instead, become a favourite choice for harvest festivals.

For the beauty of the earth,
For the beauty of the skies,
For the love which from our birth
Over and around us lies:

Christ our God, to Thee we raise
This our sacrifice of praise.

For the beauty of each hour
For the day and of the night,
Hill and vale, and tree and flower,
Sun and moon, and stars of light:

For the joy of ear and eye,
For the heart and mind's delight,
For the mystic harmony
Linking sense to sound and sight:

For the joy of human love,
Brother, sister, parent, child,
Friends on earth, and friends above,
For all gentle thoughts and mild:

For each perfect gift of thine
To our race so freely given,
Graces human and divine,
Flowers of earth and buds of heaven:

For Thy church that evermore
Lifteth holy hands above,
Offering up on every shore
This pure sacrifice of love:

Folliott Sandford Pierpoint (1836–1917)

For unto us a child is born

This biblical passage, from Isaiah 9:2–7, is a popular choice of reading at Christmas time. It is doubly familiar today from the use composer George Frideric Handel made of it in his great 'Hallelujah Chorus' from his oratorio Messiah *(1742). Handel himself described how the inspiration for the 'Hallelujah Chorus' came to him in visionary terms: 'I saw the Heavens opened, and the Great white God sitting on the Throne … whether I was in my body or out of my body as I wrote it I know not. God knows.'*

The people who walked in darkness have seen a great light;
those who lived in a land of deep darkness
– on them light has shined.
You have multiplied the nation, you have increased its joy;
they rejoice before you as with joy at the harvest,
as people exult when dividing plunder.
For the yoke of their burden,
and the bar across their shoulders,
the rod of their oppressor,
you have broken as on the day of Midian.
For all the boots of the tramping warriors
and all the garments rolled in blood
shall be burned as fuel for the fire.
For a child has been born for us, a son given to us;
authority rests upon his shoulders; and he is named
Wonderful Counsellor, Mighty God, Everlasting Father,
Prince of Peace.
His authority shall grow continually, and there shall be endless peace
for the throne of David and his kingdom.
He will establish and uphold it
with justice and with righteousness
from this time onwards and for evermore.
The zeal of the LORD of hosts will do this.

Friends, Romans, countrymen

The biting address delivered by Antony over the murdered Caesar in William Shakespeare's Julius Caesar *(1599), III, ii, ranks among the playwright's most celebrated creations. Lines from it are often quoted at funerals and on other public occasions, although the penetrating criticisms of Caesar's murderers within the passage mean that it is rarely quoted in full except within the context of the play itself.*

Friends, Romans, countrymen, lend me your ears;
I come to bury Caesar, not to praise him.
The evil that men do lives after them;
The good is oft interred with their bones:
So let it be with Caesar.
Here, under leave of Brutus and the rest
(For Brutus is an honourable man;
So are they all, all honourable men),
Come I to speak in Caesar's funeral.
He was my friend, faithful and just to me;
But Brutus says he was ambitious,
And Brutus is an honourable man.
He hath brought many captives home to Rome,
Whose ransoms did the general coffers fill:
Did this in Caesar seem ambitious?
When that the poor have cried Caesar hath wept;
Ambition should be made of sterner stuff;
Yet Brutus says he was ambitious,
And Brutus is an honourable man.
I speak not to disprove what Brutus spoke,
But here I am to speak what I do know.
You all did love him once, not without cause;
What cause withholds you, then, to mourn for him?
O judgment, thou art fled to brutish beasts,
And men have lost their reason! Bear with me;
My heart is in the coffin there with Caesar,
And I must pause till it come back to me...

... If you have tears, prepare to shed them now.
You all do know this mantle: I remember
The first time ever Caesar put it on;
Twas on a summer's evening, in his tent,
That day he overcame the Nervii:
Look! In this place ran Cassius' dagger through:
See what a rent the envious Casca made:
Through this the well-beloved Brutus stabbed;
And, as he plucked his cursed steel away,
Mark how the blood of Caesar followed it,
As rushing out of doors, to be resolved
If Brutus so unkindly knocked, or no;
For Brutus, as you know, was Caesar's angel:
Judge, O you gods, how dearly Caesar loved him!
This was the most unkindest cut of all:
For when the noble Caesar saw him stab,
Ingratitude, more strong than traitors' arms,
Quite vanquished him; then burst his mighty heart;
And, in his mantle muffling up his face,
Even at the base of Pompey's statue,
Which all the while ran blood, great Caesar fell.
O, what a fall was there, my countrymen!

William Shakespeare (1564–1616)

Give a man a horse

This poem by the Scottish poet James Thomson ranks among his best-loved verse. It is sometimes recited at wedding celebrations.

Give a man a horse he can ride,
Give a man a boat he can sail,
And his rank and wealth, his strength and health,
Nor sea nor shore shall fail.

Give a man a pipe he can smoke,
Give a man a book he can read,
And his home is bright with a calm delight,
Though the rooms be poor indeed.

Give a man a girl he can love,
As I, O my Love, love thee,
And his hand is great with the pulse of Fate,
At home, on land, on sea.

James Thomson (1700–48)

Glorious things of thee are spoken

John Newton had a surprising background for a hymn writer, having been an atheist and a slave-trader before turning to the church and ultimately being ordained in 1764. Press-ganged into the navy at 17, he led a dissolute life until the trauma of a terrible storm at sea prompted him to change his ways. As curate at Olney in Northamptonshire he formed a creative partnership with the poet William Cowper and produced with him the celebrated Olney Hymns *(1779). Although now often sung to Cyril Taylor's 'Abbot's Leigh', the traditional choice of tune to accompany these words is Joseph Haydn's 'Austria', which was also that of the Austrian and German national anthem – hence Kaiser Wilhelm's bemusement when his godmother Queen Victoria asked for it to be played at morning service during one of his visits to Windsor Castle.*

Glorious things of thee are spoken,
Zion, city of our God;
He whose word cannot be broken
Formed thee for His own abode.
On the Rock of Ages founded,
What can shake thy sure repose?
With salvation's walls surrounded,
Thou may'st smile at all thy foes.

See, the streams of living waters,
Springing from eternal love,
Well supply thy sons and daughters,
And all fear of want remove:
Who can faint, while such a river
Ever flows their thirst to assuage?
Grace, which like the LORD the giver,
Never fails from age to age.

Saviour, if of Zion's city
I, through grace, a member am,
Let the world deride or pity,
I will glory in Thy name:
Fading is the worldling's pleasure,
All his boasted pomp and show;
Solid joys and lasting treasure
None but Zion's children know.

John Newton (1725–1807)

God be in my head

No one knows who was the original author of these lines, which first appeared in the form of a prayer in the Sarum Primer (1514). As a prayer it became well known during the reign of Henry VIII and was subsequently set to music by several composers, notably Sir Walford Davies (1869–1941), whose tune is now the standard setting.

God be in my head,
And in my understanding;
God be in my eyes,
And in my looking;
God be in my mouth,
And in my speaking;
God be in my heart,
And in my thinking;
God be at my end,
And at my departing.

Anonymous

God is our refuge and strength

This biblical passage, found at Psalm 46:1–11, is often drawn upon as a source of reassurance in times of difficulty. As such, it is one of the most familiar parts of the Bible.

God is our refuge and strength,
  a very present help in trouble.
Therefore we will not fear, though the earth should change,
  though the mountains shake in the heart of the sea;
though its waters roar and foam,
  though the mountains tremble with its tumult. *Selah*
There is a river whose streams make glad the city of God,
  the holy habitation of the Most High.
God is in the midst of the city; it shall not be moved;
  God will help it when the morning dawns.
The nations are in an uproar, the kingdoms totter;
  he utters his voice, the earth melts.
The Lord of hosts is with us;
  the God of Jacob is our refuge. *Selah*
Come, behold the works of the Lord;
  see what destructions he has brought on the earth.
He makes wars cease to the ends of the earth;
  he breaks the bow, and shatters the spear;
  he burns the shields with fire.
"Be still, and know that I am God!
  I am exalted among the nations,
  I am exalted in the earth."
The Lord of hosts is with us;
  the God of Jacob is our refuge.

God moves in a mysterious way

More than many other hymns, this particular work with its anguished message of hope closely reflected the inner turmoil of its creator. The poet William Cowper suffered many crises during his life, ranging from the premature death of his mother to his being prevented from marrying the girl he loved. He turned to hymn writing after a mental breakdown and a year in an insane asylum. He found spiritual solace in compiling with John Newton the celebrated Olney Hymns *(1779) and this hymn was the last one contributed by Cowper before his mental problems resurfaced in 1773; he never recovered. One tradition insists that Cowper wrote the hymn after a failed suicide attempt.*

God moves in a mysterious way
His wonders to perform;
He plants His footsteps in the sea,
And rides upon the storm.

Deep in unfathomable mines
Of never-failing skill
He treasures up His bright designs,
And works His sovereign will.

Ye fearful saints, fresh courage take,
The clouds ye so much dread
Are big with mercy, and shall break
In blessings on your head.

Judge not the LORD by feeble sense,
But trust Him for His grace;
Behind a frowning providence
He hides a smiling face.

His purposes will ripen fast,
Unfolding every hour;
The bud may have a bitter taste,
But sweet will be the flower.

Blind unbelief is sure to err,
And scan His work in vain;
God is His own interpreter,
And He will make it plain.

William Cowper (1731–1800)

God save the queen

The authorship of the British national anthem (which becomes 'God save the king' when the monarch is male) is often credited to Dr John Bull (d.1628), English organist at Antwerp cathedral, although other suggestions claim that it was the work of French composer Jean Baptiste Lully (1632–87). It is sometimes also attributed (less reliably) to English poet and musician Henry Carey (c.1690–1743) whose other well-known work was the song 'Sally in our alley'. The words would seem to have been inspired by a quotation from the Bible: 'And all the people shouted, and said, God save the king' (1 Samuel 10:24). On most occasions only the first verse is sung, although the third verse is also sometimes added. The sixth verse, never sung today, is a reminder that when the full anthem was first publicly performed, in London in 1745, the Jacobite Rebellion was then taking place in Scotland.

God save our gracious queen,
Long live our noble queen,
God save the queen!
Send her victorious,
Happy and glorious,
Long to reign over us;
God save the queen!

O Lord our God arise,
Scatter her enemies
And make them fall;
Confound their politics,
Frustrate their knavish tricks,
On Thee our hopes we fix,
God save us all!

Thy choicest gifts in store
On her be pleased to pour;
Long may she reign;
May she defend our laws,
And ever give us cause
To sing with heart and voice,
God save the queen!

Not in this land alone,
But be God's mercies known,
From shore to shore!
Lord make the nations see,
That men should brothers be,
And form one family,
The wide world over.

From every latent foe,
From the assassins blow,
God save the queen!
O'er her thine arm extend,
For Britain's sake defend,
Our mother, prince, and friend,
God save the queen!

Lord grant that Marshal Wade
May by thy mighty aid
Victory bring.
May he sedition hush,
And like a torrent rush,
Rebellious Scots to crush.
God save the king!

Anonymous

God's grandeur

Gerard Manley Hopkins was received into the Roman Catholic church in 1866 and for many years was troubled by the thought that his poetry conflicted with his religious faith. He symbolically burned many of his poems on becoming a Jesuit in 1868, but later resumed his poetic career, his spiritual convictions providing the bedrock of his inspiration. These lines celebrating God's presence in the world are typical, combining religious sentiment with literary virtuosity.

The world is charged with the grandeur of God.
It will flame out, like shining from shook foil;
It gathers to a greatness, like the ooze of oil
Crushed. Why do men then now not reck his rod?
Generations have trod, have trod, have trod;
And all is seared with trade; bleared, smeared with toil;
And wears man's smudge and shares man's smell: the soil
Is bare now, nor can foot feel, being shod.

And for all this, nature is never spent;
There lives the dearest freshness deep down things;
And though the last lights off the black West went
Oh, morning, at the brown brink eastward, springs –
Because the Holy Ghost over the bent
World broods with warm breast and with ah! bright wings.

Gerard Manley Hopkins (1844–89)

The Good Samaritan

The parable of the Good Samaritan, as related at Luke 10:25–37, is one of the best-loved parables in the Bible. The Samaritans were open enemies of the Jews and so this tale of compassion shown by a passing Samaritan to an injured Jew is especially striking.

Just then a lawyer stood up to test Jesus. 'Teacher,' he said, 'what must I do to inherit eternal life?' He said to him, 'What is written in the law? What do you read there?' He answered, 'You shall love the LORD your God with all your heart, and with all your soul, and with all your strength, and with all your mind; and your neighbour as yourself.' And he said to him, 'You have given the right answer; do this, and you will live.'

But wanting to justify himself, he asked Jesus, 'And who is my neighbour?' Jesus replied, 'A man was going down from Jerusalem to Jericho, and fell into the hands of robbers, who stripped him, beat him, and went away, leaving him half dead. Now by chance a priest was going down that road; and when he saw him, he passed by on the other side. So likewise a Levite, when he came to the place and saw him, passed by on the other side. But a Samaritan while travelling came near him; and when he saw him, he was moved with pity. He went to him and bandaged his wounds, having poured oil and wine on them. Then he put him on his own animal, brought him to an inn, and took care of him. The next day he took out two denarii, gave them to the innkeeper, and said, "Take care of him; and when I come back, I will repay you whatever more you spend." Which of these three, do you think, was a neighbour to the man who fell into the hands of the robbers?' He said, 'The one who showed him mercy.' Jesus said to him, 'Go and do likewise.'

Great is thy faithfulness

Thomas Obadiah Chisholm was an impoverished insurance agent who was obliged by ill health to give up as a Methodist minister after only a year. A life of disappointment and poor health never reduced Chisholm's faithfulness, as evidenced by this hymn and his own observation in his old age of God that 'He has given me many wonderful displays of His providing care, for which I am filled with astonishing gratefulness.'

Great is Thy faithfulness, O God my Father,
There is no shadow of turning with Thee;
Thou changest not, Thy compassions, they fail not;
As Thou hast been Thou for ever wilt be.

Great is Thy faithfulness, great is Thy faithfulness,
Morning by morning new mercies I see;
All I have needed Thy hand hath provided,
Great is Thy faithfulness, Lord, unto me.

Summer and winter, and springtime and harvest,
Sun, moon and stars in their courses above,
Join with all nature in manifold witness
To Thy great faithfulness, mercy and love.

Pardon for sin and a peace that endureth,
Thine own dear presence to cheer and to guide;
Strength for today and bright hope for tomorrow,
Blessings all mine, with ten thousand beside!

Thomas Obadiah Chisholm (1866–1960)

Guide me, O Thou great Redeemer

The most popular of all Welsh hymns, 'Guide me, O Thou great Redeemer/Jehovah' is a perennial favourite among Welsh singers both inside and outside church. William Williams and Peter Williams were not related. William Williams was nicknamed the 'Sweet Singer' of Pantycelyn and was ordained into the Anglican Church before joining the Methodists. Peter Williams was an Anglican clergyman who similarly joined the Methodists and translated William Williams' lines into English. 'Cwm Rhondda', the tune to which the lines have been sung since 1905, was the work of John Hughes, a dedicated chapelgoer who spent his life working firstly in a colliery and subsequently for the Great Western Railway.

Guide me, O Thou great Redeemer,
Pilgrim through this barren land;
I am weak, but Thou art mighty,
Hold me with Thy powerful hand:
Bread of heaven,
Feed me till I want no more.

Open now the crystal fountain
Whence the healing stream doth flow;
Let the fire and cloudy pillar
Lead me all my journey through:
Strong deliverer,
Be Thou still my strength and shield.

When I tread the verge of Jordan,
Bid my anxious fears subside;
Death of death, and hell's destruction,
Land me safe on Canaan's side:
Songs of praises
I will ever give to Thee.

William Williams (1717–91) and Peter Williams (1727–96)

Hallelujah, what a Saviour!

Philipp Bliss, American hymn writer, wrote the words and music for a number of hymns that are still well known today. He refused to profit from his work and gave the substantial sums due in royalties to charity. Shortly after Christmas 1876 he set out with his wife for Chicago, passengers in the ill-fated train that broke through the bridge across the Ashtabula River, plunging seventy feet and burning. Neither he nor his wife escaped the disaster.

'Man of Sorrows!' what a name
For the Son of God who came
Ruined sinners to reclaim!
Hallelujah! What a Saviour!

Bearing shame and scoffing rude,
In my place condemned He stood;
Sealed my pardon with His blood:
Hallelujah! What a Saviour!

Guilty, vile and helpless, we
Spotless Lamb of God was He:
Full atonement! – can it be?
Hallelujah! What a Saviour!

Lifted up was He to die,
'It is finished,' was His cry;
Now in heaven exalted high:
Hallelujah! What a Saviour!

When He comes, our glorious King,
All His ransomed home to bring,
Then anew this song we'll sing:
Hallelujah! What a Saviour!

P. P. Bliss (1838–76)

Hark! the herald-angels sing

Charles Wesley, who with his brother John founded the Methodist Church, is recognized as the most admired and prolific of hymn writers, with some 8000 compositions to his credit. As well as the rousing 'Hark! the herald-angels sing', one of the most familiar of all Christmas carols, he was the author of such much-loved hymns as 'Jesu, lover of my soul' and 'Love divine, all loves excelling'.

Hark! the herald-angels sing
Glory to the new-born King,
Peace on earth, and mercy mild,
God and sinners reconciled.
Joyful, all ye nations rise,
Join the triumph of the skies;
With the angelic host proclaim,
'Christ is born in Bethlehem.'

Hark! the herald-angels sing
Glory to the new-born King.

Christ, by highest heaven adored,
Christ, the everlasting LORD,
Late in time behold Him come,
Offspring of a virgin's womb.
Veiled in flesh the Godhead see!
Hail, the incarnate deity!
Pleased as man with man to dwell,
Jesus, our Emmanuel.

Hail, the heaven-born Prince of peace!
Hail, the sun of righteousness!
Light and life to all He brings,
Risen with healing in His wings,
Mild He lays His glory by,
Born that man no more may die,
Born to raise the sons of earth,
Born to give them second birth.

Charles Wesley (1707–88)

Hills of the north, rejoice

Charles Edward Oakley was rector at Wickwar in Gloucestershire and subsequently at St Paul's, Covent Garden. 'Hills of the north, rejoice' was, it seems, his one and only contribution to hymn writing, but it has remained nonetheless a perennial favourite, albeit in amended form (the original including such contentious phrases as 'the heathen in his blindness').

Hills of the north, rejoice,
River and mountain-spring,
Hark to the advent voice;
Valley and lowland, sing.
Christ comes in righteousness and love,
He brings salvation from above.

Isles of the southern seas,
Sing to the listening earth;
Carry on every breeze
Hope of a world's new birth:
In Christ shall all be made anew;
His word is sure, His promise true.

Lands of the East, arise,
He is your brightest morn,
Greet him with joyous eyes,
Praise shall His path adorn:
The God whom you have longed to know
In Christ draws near, and calls you now.

Shores of the utmost west,
Lands of the setting sun,
Welcome the heavenly guest
In whom the dawn has come:
He brings a never-ending light,
Who triumphed o'er our darkest night.

Shout, as you journey home;
Songs be in every mouth!
Lo, from the north they come,
From east and west and south:
In Jesus all shall find their rest,
In Him the universe be blest.

Charles Edward Oakley (1832–65)

Holy, holy, holy! Lord God Almighty

Reginald Heber, a vicar at Hodnet in Shropshire before becoming bishop of Calcutta at the age of just 39, composed the following lines (first published in 1811) for performance on Trinity Sunday. Admirers of the hymn over the years have included Alfred, Lord Tennyson, who declared it the greatest hymn in the English language.

Holy, holy, holy! Lord God Almighty!
Early in the morning our song shall rise to Thee;
Holy, holy, holy! Merciful and mighty,
God in three Persons, blessed Trinity!

Holy, holy, holy! All the saints adore Thee,
Casting down their golden crowns around the glassy sea;
Cherubim and seraphim falling down before Thee,
Which wert, and art, and evermore shalt be.

Holy, holy, holy! Though the darkness hide Thee,
Though the eye of sinful man Thy glory may not see,
Only Thou art holy, there is none beside Thee
Perfect in power, in love, and purity.

Holy, holy, holy! Lord God Almighty,
All Thy works shall praise Thy name, in earth,
and sky, and sea;
Holy, holy, holy! Merciful and mighty!
God in three Persons, blessed Trinity!

Reginald Heber (1783–1826)

Home, sweet home

John Howard Payne was a US actor and playwright who also served far away from home as US consul in Tunis. This celebrated expression of sentiment towards home and hearth comes from his play Clari, The Maid of Milan. *Payne's words were set to music by Sir Henry Bishop and the resulting ditty became a great favourite among Victorian parlour songs, long outliving the popularity of the play from which it originally came.*

Mid pleasures and palaces though we may roam,
Be it ever so humble, there's no place like home!
A charm from the skies seems to hallow us there,
Which, seek through the world, is ne'er met with elsewhere.

An exile from home, splendour dazzles in vain!
Oh, give me my lowly thatched cottage again!
The birds singing gaily that came at my call,
Give me them, and the peace of mind dearer than all!

Home, home, sweet, sweet home!
There's no place like home! there's no place like home!

John Howard Payne (1791–1852)

Home-thoughts, from abroad

The patriotic appeal of this poem by Robert Browning has kept it a popular favourite into modern times. The nostalgia for the home country from abroad has particular resonance through its relevance to the author's own life, which famously included years of exile in Italy after he secretly eloped in 1846 with fellow-poet Elizabeth Barrett in defiance of the wishes of her father.

Oh, to be in England
Now that April's there,
And whoever wakes in England
Sees, some morning, unaware,
That the lowest boughs and the brushwood sheaf
Round the elm-tree bole are in tiny leaf,
While the chaffinch sings on the orchard bough
In England – now!

And after April, when May follows,
And the whitethroat builds, and all the swallows –
Hark! where my blossomed pear-tree in the hedge
Leans to the field and scatters on the clover
Blossoms and dewdrops – at the bent spray's edge –
That's the wise thrush; he sings each song twice over,
Lest you should think he never could recapture
The first fine careless rapture!
And though the fields look rough with hoary dew,
All will be gay when noontide wakes anew
The buttercups, the little children's dower,
– Far brighter than this gaudy melon-flower!

Robert Browning (1812–89)

The hound of heaven

This memorable poem by the eccentric poet-tramp Francis Thompson dramatizes the flight of the soul from pursuit by the Holy Spirit. Thompson himself was born into a respectable Catholic family but experienced hard times as a homeless, opium-addicted wanderer of the streets of London before finding shelter ultimately with the family of a Catholic publisher.

I fled Him, down the nights and down the days;
I fled Him down the arches of the years;
I fled Him, down the labyrinthine ways
Of my own mind; and in the mist of tears
I hid from Him, and under running laughter.
    Up vistaed hopes I sped;
    And shot, precipitated.
Adown Titanic glooms of chasmed fears,
From those strong Feet that followed, followed after.
    But with unhurrying chase,
    And unperturbed pace,
Deliberate speed, majestic instancy
    They beat – and a Voice beat
    More instant than the Feet –
'All things betray thee, who betrayest Me.'

    I pleaded, outlaw-wise,
By many a hearted casement, curtained red,
    Trellised with intertwining charities;
(For, though I knew his love Who followed,
    Yet was I sore adread
Lest, having Him, I must have naught beside);
But, if one little casement parted wide,
    The gust of his approach would clash it to.
Fear wist not to evade, as Love wist to pursue.
Across the margent of the world I fled,
    And troubled the gold gateways of the stars,
    Smiting for shelter on their clanged bars;
    Fretted to dulcet jars
And silvern chatter the pale ports o' the moon.
I said to dawn, Be sudden; to eve, Be soon;
    With thy young skiey blossoms heap me over

From this tremendous Lover!
Float thy vague veil about me, lest He see!
I tempted all His servitors, but to find
My own betrayal in their constancy,
In faith to Him their fickleness to me,
Their traitorous trueness, and their loyal deceit.
To all swift things for swiftness did I sue;
Clung to the whistling mane of every wind.
But whether, they swept, smoothly fleet,
The long savannahs of the blue;
Or whether, Thunder-driven,
They clanged his chariot 'thwart a heaven
Plashy with flying lightnings round the spurn o' their feet:
Fear wist not to evade as Love wist to pursue.
Still with unhurrying chase,
And perturbed pace,
Deliberate speed, majestic instancy,
Came on the following Feet,
And a Voice above their beat –
'Naught shelters thee, who wilt not shelter Me.'

Now of that long pursuit
Comes on at hand the bruit:
That Voice is round me like a bursting sea:
'And is thy earth so marred,
Shattered in shard on shard?
Lo, all things fly thee, for thou fliest Me!
Strange, piteous, futile thing,
Wherefore should any set thee love apart?
Seeing none but I makes much of naught' (He said)
And human love needs human meriting:
How hast thou merited –
Of all man's clotted clay the dingiest clot?
Alack, thou knowest not
How little worthy of any love thou art!
Whom wilt thou find to love ignoble thee
Save Me, save only Me?
All which I took from thee I did but take,

Not for thy harms,
But just that thou might'st seek it in My arms.
All which thy child's mistake
Fancies as lost, I have stored for thee at home:
Rise, clasp My hand, and come!'

Halts by me that footfall:
Is my gloom, after all,
Shade of His hand, outstretched caressingly?
'Ah, fondest, blindest, weakest,
I am He Whom thou seekest!
Thou dravest love from thee, who dravest Me.'

Francis Thompson (1859–1907)

How do I love thee? Let me count the ways

The English poet Elizabeth Barrett Browning wrote 'Sonnet 43', one of the Sonnets from the Portuguese *(1850), following her elopement with fellow-writer Robert Browning in 1846. The fraught circumstances surrounding their union, in the face of fierce opposition from Elizabeth Barrett's father and her own long-term invalidity, are well-known and this particular poem has become a favourite expression of loving devotion, often recited at weddings.*

How do I love thee? Let me count the ways.
I love thee to the depth and breadth and height
My soul can reach, when feeling out of sight
For the ends of Being and ideal Grace.
I love thee to the level of everyday's
Most quiet need, by sun and candle-light.
I love thee freely, as men strive for Right;
I love thee purely, as they turn from Praise.
I love thee with the passion put to use
In my old griefs, and with my childhood's faith.
I love thee with a love I seemed to lose
With my lost saints, – I love thee with the breath,
Smiles, tears, of all my life! – and, if God choose,
I shall but love thee better after death.

Elizabeth Barrett Browning (1806–61)

How great Thou art!

This hymn was originally inspired by a poem, "O store Gud" ("O great God"). A Swedish pastor, Carl Boberg, wrote the poem in Monsteras in southern Sweden in 1885. Having converted to Christianity after time at sea, he was moved to write the poem following a wild thunderstorm: as the storm abated he saw a great rainbow span the Gulf of Monsteras at the same moment that the bells of the local church began to peal. Boberg's poem served as an inspiration to Stuart Hine (1899–1989), a British missionary serving in a remote part of Eastern Europe. The sentiments expressed in Boberg's poem and Hine's own personal experiences led him to write the well-known English hymn, "How Great Thou Art!". It is widely known among English speakers and was taken up by US evangelist, Billy Graham, in the 1950s.

O Lord my God, when I in awesome wonder
Consider all the works Thy hand hath made,
I see the stars, I hear the mighty thunder,
Thy power throughout the universe displayed:

Then sings my soul, my Saviour God, to Thee,
How great Thou art, how great Thou art!
Then sings my soul, my Saviour God, to Thee,
How great Thou art, how great Thou art!

When through the woods and forest glades I wander
And hear the birds sing sweetly in the trees;
When I look down from lofty mountain grandeur,
And hear the brook, and feel the gentle breeze;

And when I think that God his Son not sparing,
Sent Him to die – I scarce can take it in,
That on the cross, my burden gladly bearing,
He bled and died to take away my sin:

When Christ shall come with shout of acclamation
And take me home – what joy shall fill my heart!
Then shall I bow in humble adoration,
And there proclaim, my God, how great Thou art!

Carl Boberg (1859–1940)

How sweet the name of Jesus sounds

This hymn was originally published as one of the Olney Hymns *(1779) written by William Cowper and John Newton. Although Cowper's is perhaps the more famous name, he only contributed 68 of the hymns, the remaining 280 being the work of Newton (amongst them such classics as 'Glorious things of thee are spoken'). The title of the hymn comes from the Song of Solomon 1:3, which runs 'Thy name is as ointment poured forth.'*

How sweet the name of Jesus sounds
In a believer's ear!
It soothes our sorrows, heals our wounds,
And drives away our fear.

It makes the wounded spirit whole,
And calms the troubled breast;
'Tis manna to the hungry soul,
And to the weary rest.

Dear name! the rock on which I build,
My shield and hiding-place,
My never-failing treasury filled
With boundless stores of grace.

Jesus! my Shepherd, Brother, Friend,
My Prophet, Priest, and King,
My Lord, my Life, my Way, my End,
Accept the praise I bring.

Weak is the effort of my heart,
And cold my warmest thought;
But when I see Thee as Thou art,
I'll praise Thee as I ought.

Till then I would Thy love proclaim
With every fleeting breath;
And may the music of Thy Name
Refresh my soul in death.

John Newton (1725–1807)

I am the good shepherd

The picture of Christ as a shepherd tending his flock is among the most cherished of biblical metaphors. Jesus himself develops it in this passage from John 10:1-18, which remains one of the best-loved readings from the Bible.

'Very truly, I tell you, anyone who does not enter the sheepfold by the gate but climbs in by another way is a thief and a bandit. The one who enters by the gate is the shepherd of the sheep. The gatekeeper opens the gate for him, and the sheep hear his voice. He calls his own sheep by name and leads them out. When he has brought out all his own, he goes ahead of them, and the sheep follow him because they know his voice. They will not follow a stranger, but they will run from him because they do not know the voice of strangers.' Jesus used this figure of speech with them, but they did not understand what he was saying to them.

So again Jesus said to them, 'Very truly, I tell you, I am the gate for the sheep. All who came before me are thieves and bandits; but the sheep did not listen to them. I am the gate. Whoever enters by me will be saved, and will come in and go out and find pasture. The thief comes only to steal and kill and destroy. I came that they may have life, and have it abundantly.

'I am the good shepherd. The good shepherd lays down his life for the sheep. The hired hand, who is not the shepherd and does not own the sheep, sees the wolf coming and leaves the sheep and runs away – and the wolf snatches them and scatters them. The hired hand runs away because a hired hand does not care for the sheep. I am the good shepherd. I know my own and my own know me, just as the Father knows me and I know the Father. And I lay down my life for the sheep. I have other sheep that do not belong to this fold. I must bring them also, and they will listen to my voice. So there will be one flock, one shepherd. For this reason the Father loves me, because I lay down my life in order to take it up again. No one takes it from me, but I lay it down of my own accord. I have power to lay it down, and I have power to take it up again. I have received this command from my Father.'

I am the resurrection and the life

The story of Lazarus is related at John 11:17–27 and 38–44. Offering proof of Christ's triumph over death, it has long been a favourite Bible reading.

When Jesus arrived, he found that Lazarus had already been in the tomb for four days. Now Bethany was near Jerusalem, some two miles away, and many of the Jews had come to Martha and Mary to console them about their brother. When Martha heard that Jesus was coming, she went and met him, while Mary stayed at home. Martha said to Jesus, 'LORD, if you had been here, my brother would not have died. But even now I know that God will give you whatever you ask of him.' Jesus said to her, 'Your brother will rise again.' Martha said to him, 'I know that he will rise again in the resurrection on the last day.' Jesus said to her, 'I am the resurrection and the life. Those who believe in me, even though they die, will live, and everyone who lives and believes in me will never die. Do you believe this?' She said to him, 'Yes, Lord, I believe that you are the Messiah, the Son of God, the one coming into the world.'

Then Jesus, again greatly disturbed, came to the tomb. It was a cave, and a stone was lying against it. Jesus said, 'Take away the stone.' Martha, the sister of the dead man, said to him, 'LORD, already there is a stench because he has been dead for four days.' Jesus said to her, 'Did I not tell you that if you believed, you would see the glory of God?' So they took away the stone. And Jesus looked upwards and said, 'Father, I thank you for having heard me. I knew that you always hear me, but I have said this for the sake of the crowd standing here, so that they may believe that you sent me.'

When he had said this, he cried with a loud voice, 'Lazarus, come out!' The dead man came out, his hands and feet bound with strips of cloth, and his face wrapped in a cloth. Jesus said to them, 'Unbind him, and let him go.'

I felt my heart strangely warmed

The following extracts from the Journal *of John Wesley are among the most famous lines he ever wrote. They describe the moment of revelation that assured him of the reality of salvation and prompted him to embark upon his great evangelistic mission, from which evolved the Methodist Church. On 24 May 1738, John fully accepted Jesus as his Saviour after a religious experience in Aldersgate Street meeting house, where he felt his heart 'strangely warmed' by the love of God. From then on, John travelled all over England preaching that a person could know God's grace fully and live a life based upon Christian love.*

Wed. May 24. – I think it was about five this morning that I opened my Testament on those words, "There are given unto us exceeding great and precious promises, even that ye should be partakers of the divine nature" (2 Peter 1:4). Just as I went out, I opened it again on those words, "Thou art not far from the kingdom of God." In the afternoon I was asked to go to St Paul's. The anthem was, "Out of the deep have I called unto thee, O Lord: Lord, hear my voice. O let thine ears consider well the voice of my complaint. If thou, Lord, wilt be extreme to mark what is done amiss, O Lord, who may abide it? For there is mercy with thee; therefore shalt thou be feared. O Israel, trust in the Lord: for with the Lord there is mercy, and with Him is plenteous redemption. And He shall redeem Israel from all his sins."

In the evening I went very unwillingly to a society in Aldersgate street, where one was reading Luther's preface to the Epistle to the Romans. About a quarter before nine, while he was describing the change which God works in the heart through faith in Christ, I felt my heart strangely warmed. I felt I did trust in Christ, Christ alone, for salvation; and an assurance was given me that He had taken away my sins, even mine, and saved me from the law of sin and death.

I began to pray with all my might for those who had in a more especial manner despitefully used me and persecuted me. I then testified openly to all there what I now first felt in my heart. But it was not long before the enemy suggested, "This cannot be faith; for where is thy joy?" Then was I taught that peace and victory over sin are essential to faith in the Captain of our salvation; but that, as to the transports of joy that usually attend the beginning of it, especially in those who have mourned deeply, God sometimes giveth, sometimes withholdeth them, according to the counsels of His own will.

After my return home, I was much buffeted with temptations; but cried out, and they fled away. They returned again and again. I as often lifted up my eyes, and He sent me help from His holy place. And herein I found the difference between this and my former state chiefly consisted. I was striving, yea, fighting with all my might under the law, as well as under grace. But then I was sometimes, if not often, conquered; now, I was always conqueror.

Thur. 25. – The moment I awaked, "Jesus, Master," was in my heart and in my mouth; and I found all my strength lay in keeping my eye fixed upon Him, and my soul waiting on Him continually. Being again at St. Paul's in the afternoon, I could taste the good word of God in the anthem, which began, "My song shall be always of the loving-kindness of the Lord: with my mouth will I ever be showing forth thy truth from one generation to another." Yet the enemy injected a fear, "If thou dost believe, why is there not a more sensible change?" I answered (yet not I), "That I know not. But this I know, I have now peace with God. And I sin not to-day, and Jesus my Master has forbid me to take thought for the morrow."

John Wesley (1703–91)

I run toward the prize

This consolatory passage from Philippians 3:8–14 is sometimes recited at funerals to remind the faithful that, for those who truly believe, death is but a rite of passage towards an infinitely greater life.

More than that, I regard everything as loss because of the surpassing value of knowing Christ Jesus my LORD. For his sake I have suffered the loss of all things, and I regard them as rubbish, in order that I may gain Christ and be found in him, not having a righteousness of my own that comes from the law, but one that comes through faith in Christ, the righteousness from God based on faith. I want to know Christ and the power of his resurrection and the sharing of his sufferings by becoming like him in his death, if somehow I may attain the resurrection from the dead.

Not that I have already obtained this or have already reached the goal; but I press on to make it my own, because Christ Jesus has made me his own. Beloved, I do not consider that I have made it my own; but this one thing I do: forgetting what lies behind and straining forward to what lies ahead, I press on towards the goal for the prize of the heavenly call of God in Christ Jesus.

I've found a friend

James Small was a minister in the Scottish Free Church and the author of several popular hymns, which were published in Hymns for Youthful Voices *(1859) and subsequent volumes. The original title of the hymn was 'Jesus the Friend'.*

I've found a friend, O such a friend!
He loved me ere I knew Him;
He drew me with the cords of love,
And thus He bound me to Him.
And round my heart still closely twine
Those ties which naught can sever;
For I am His, and He is mine,
Forever and forever.

I've found a friend; O such a friend!
He bled, He died to save me;
And not alone the gift of life,
But His own self He gave me.
Naught that I have my own I call,
I hold it for the Giver;
My heart, my strength, my life, my all,
Are His, and His forever.

I've found a friend; O such a friend!
So kind and true and tender;
So wise a counsellor and guide,
So mighty a defender!
From Him who loves me now so well,
What power my soul shall sever?
Shall life or death, shall earth or hell?
No; I am His forever.

James Grindlay Small (1817–88)

I vow to thee, my country

This patriotic hymn was written by Cecil Spring-Rice, a prominent member of Britain's diplomatic corps. The heavy casualties of World War I, during much of which Spring-Rice served as Ambassador to Washington, led him to tone down the overtly patriotic sentiment of the original version and to emphasize the good Christian's citizenship of two countries – those of his earthly homeland and of heaven above – but his most famous hymn has still been criticized from time to time for its jingoistic overtones. It received renewed attention in 1981 when it was selected as part of the wedding service of Prince Charles and Lady Diana Spencer at St Paul's Cathedral.

I vow to thee, my country, all earthly things above,
Entire and whole and perfect, the service of my love:
The love that asks no questions, the love that stands the test,
That lays upon the altar the dearest and the best;
The love that never falters, the love that pays the price,
The love that makes undaunted the final sacrifice.

And there's another country, I've heard of long ago,
Most dear to them that love her, most great to them that
know;
We may not count her armies, we may not see her King;
Her fortress is a faithful heart, her pride is suffering;
And soul by soul and silently her shining bounds increase,
And her ways are ways of gentleness and all her paths are
peace.

Cecil Spring-Rice (1859–1918)

I wandered lonely as a cloud

William Wordsworth's untitled poem variously referred to as 'I wandered lonely as a cloud' or 'Daffodils' may claim to be the single best-known poem in the English language. It was written in 1804 and remains a hugely popular celebration of the English countryside in spring.

I wandered lonely as a cloud
That floats on high o'er vales and hills,
When all at once I saw a crowd,
A host, of golden daffodils;
Beside the lake, beneath the trees,
Fluttering and dancing in the breeze.

Continuous as the stars that shine
And twinkle on the Milky Way,
They stretched in never-ending line
Along the margin of a bay:
Ten thousand saw I at a glance,
Tossing their heads in sprightly dance.

The waves beside them danced; but they
Out-did the sparkling waves in glee:
A poet could not but be gay,
In such a jocund company:
I gazed, and gazed, but little thought
What wealth the show to me had brought:

For oft, when on my couch I lie
In vacant or in pensive mood,
They flash upon that inward eye
Which is the bliss of solitude;
And then my heart with pleasure fills,
And dances with the daffodils.

William Wordsworth (1770–1850)

I will lift up mine eyes unto the hills

This biblical passage, from Psalm 121:1–8, is a popular choice of reading throughout the year and at various special occasions.

I will lift up mine eyes unto the hills,
from whence cometh my help.
My help cometh from the LORD,
which made heaven and earth.

He will not suffer thy foot to be moved:
he that keepeth thee will not slumber.
Behold, he that keepeth Israel
shall neither slumber nor sleep.

The LORD is thy keeper:
the LORD is thy shade upon thy right hand.
The sun shall not smite thee by day,
nor the moon by night.

The LORD shall preserve thee from all evil:
he shall preserve thy soul.
The LORD shall preserve
thy going out and thy coming in
from this time forth, and even for evermore.

(Authorized [King James] Version)

I will raise him up at the last day

This biblical passage, from John 6:39–54, is often recited at funeral services as a reminder of Christ's promise of eternal life.

And this is the will of him who sent me, that I should lose nothing of all that he has given me, but raise it up on the last day. This is indeed the will of my Father, that all who see the Son and believe in him may have eternal life; and I will raise them up on the last day.'

Then the Jews began to complain about him because he said, 'I am the bread that came down from heaven.' They were saying, 'Is not this Jesus, the son of Joseph, whose father and mother we know? How can he now say, "I have come down from heaven"?' Jesus answered them, 'Do not complain among yourselves. No one can come to me unless drawn by the Father who sent me; and I will raise that person up on the last day. It is written in the prophets, "And they shall all be taught by God." Everyone who has heard and learned from the Father comes to me. Not that anyone has seen the Father except the one who is from God; he has seen the Father. Very truly, I tell you, whoever believes has eternal life. I am the bread of life. Your ancestors ate the manna in the wilderness, and they died. This is the bread that comes down from heaven, so that one may eat of it and not die. I am the living bread that came down from heaven. Whoever eats of this bread will live forever; and the bread that I will give for the life of the world is my flesh.'

The Jews then disputed among themselves, saying, 'How can this man give us his flesh to eat?' So Jesus said to them, 'Very truly, I tell you, unless you eat the flesh of the Son of Man and drink his blood, you have no life in you. Those who eat my flesh and drink my blood have eternal life, and I will raise them up on the last day.

If

When the British public were asked to vote for their favourite poems on National Poetry Day in 1995, Rudyard Kipling's 'If' (published in 1910) emerged as a clear winner, far outstripping all others. Over the years it has been a favourite of celebrities as diverse as Kaiser Wilhelm of Germany, who kept a copy of it on his desk, British birth control campaigner Marie Stopes and Italian communist leader Antonio Gramsci.

If you can keep your head when all about you
Are losing theirs and blaming it on you,
If you can trust yourself when all men doubt you,
But make allowance for their doubting too;
If you can wait and not be tired by waiting,
Or being lied about, don't deal in lies,
Or being hated, don't give way to hating,
And yet don't look too good, nor talk too wise:

If you can dream – and not make dreams your master;
If you can think – and not make thoughts your aim;
If you can meet with Triumph and Disaster
And treat those two imposters just the same;
If you can bear to hear the truth you've spoken
Twisted by knaves to make a trap for fools,
Or watch the things you gave your life to, broken,
And stoop and build 'em up with worn-out tools:

If you can make one heap of winnings
And risk it on one turn of pitch-and-toss,
And lose, and start again at your beginnings
And never breathe a word about your loss;
If you can force your heart and nerve and sinew
To serve your turn long after they are gone,
And so hold on when there is nothing in you
Except the Will which says to them: 'Hold on!'

If you can talk with crowds and keep your virtue,
Or walk with Kings – nor lose the common touch,
If neither foes nor loving friends can hurt you,
If all men count with you, but none too much;
If you can fill the unforgiving minute
With sixty seconds' worth of distance run,
Yours is the Earth and everything that's in it,
And – which is more – you'll be a Man, my son!

Rudyard Kipling (1865–1936)

If I should go before the rest of you

Joyce Grenfell is fondly remembered as a comedienne who starred in numerous films made by the British cinema in the post-war era. Her comic gifts are also preserved in various classic recordings made of her humorous monologues. In recent years, however, her activities as a poet have attracted increasing attention. This short verse has become a popular choice of consolatory reading for funerals.

If I should go before the rest of you,
Break not a flower nor inscribe a stone.
Nor when I am gone speak in a Sunday voice,
But be the usual selves that I have known.
Weep if you must,
Parting is hell –
But life goes on,
So sing as well.

Joyce Grenfell (1910–79)

Immortal, invisible, God only wise

Walter Chalmers Smith served as Moderator of the Free Church of Scotland from 1893 and was the author of a number of hymns, but this is the only one by him that has remained a popular favourite. It appeared in 1867 and is usually sung to the old Welsh tune 'St Denio', which was itself derived from a Welsh folk song entitled 'Can Mlynedd i'nawr'.

Admirers of this hymn include Queen Elizabeth II, who requested that it be one of the hymns sung during the celebrations of her sixtieth birthday in 1986.

Immortal, invisible, God only wise,
In light inaccessible hid from our eyes,
Most blessed, most glorious, the Ancient of Days,
Almighty, victorious, Thy great name we praise.

Unresting, unhasting, and silent as light,
Nor wanting, nor wasting, Thou rulest in might;
Thy justice like mountains high soaring above
Thy clouds which are fountains of goodness and love.

To all, life Thou givest, to both great and small;
In all life Thou livest, the true life of all;
We blossom and flourish as leaves on the tree,
And wither and perish – but naught changeth Thee.

Great Father of glory, pure Father of light,
Thine angels adore Thee, all veiling their sight;
All laud we would render: O help us to see
'Tis only the splendour of light hideth Thee.

Walter Chalmers Smith (1824–1908)

In Memoriam

Poet laureate Alfred, Lord Tennyson wrote his famous long poem In Memoriam A.H.H. *in tribute to his intimate friend Arthur Henry Hallam, whose promising scholarly career was cut short by his premature death in Vienna in 1833, at the age of 22. Despairing but strongly religious in tone, passages from it are sometimes recited to console the bereaved.*

Oh, yet we trust that somehow good
Will be the final goal of ill,
To pangs of nature, sins of will,
Defects of doubt, and taints of blood;

That nothing walks with aimless feet;
That not one life shall be destroyed,
Or cast as rubbish to the void,
When God hath made the pile complete;

That not a worm is cloven in vain;
That not a moth with vain desire
Is shrivelled in a fruitless fire,
Or but subserves another's gain.

Behold, we know not anything;
I can but trust that good shall fall
At last – far off – at last, to all,
And every winter change to spring …

This truth came borne with bier and pall,
I felt it when I sorrowed most,
'Tis better to have loved and lost,
Than never to have loved at all.

Alfred, Lord Tennyson (1809–92)

In my house are many mansions

This biblical passage, from John 14:1–26, brings reassurance of divine salvation to the faithful. Verses 1–13 are sometimes selected for recital at funerals. In the Authorized (King James) Version, the Holy Spirit is called the Comforter *and in other translations* Advocate *is rendered* Counsellor.

'Do not let your hearts be troubled. Believe in God, believe also in me. In my Father's house there are many dwelling-places. If it were not so, would I have told you that I go to prepare a place for you? And if I go and prepare a place for you, I will come again and will take you to myself, so that where I am, there you may be also. And you know the way to the place where I am going.' Thomas said to him, 'Lord, we do not know where you are going. How can we know the way?' Jesus said to him, 'I am the way, and the truth, and the life. No one comes to the Father except through me. If you know me, you will know my Father also. From now on you do know him and have seen him.'

Philip said to him, 'Lord, show us the Father, and we will be satisfied.' Jesus said to him, 'Have I been with you all this time, Philip, and you still do not know me? Whoever has seen me has seen the Father. How can you say, "Show us the Father"? Do you not believe that I am in the Father and the Father is in me? The words that I say to you I do not speak on my own; but the Father who dwells in me does his works. Believe me that I am in the Father and the Father is in me; but if you do not, then believe me because of the works themselves. Very truly, I tell you, the one who believes in me will also do the works that I do and, in fact, will do greater works than these, because I am going to the Father. I will do whatever you ask in my name, so that the Father may be glorified in the Son. If in my name you ask me for anything, I will do it.

'If you love me, you will keep my commandments. And I will ask the Father, and he will give you another Advocate, to be with you for ever. This is the Spirit of truth, whom the world cannot receive, because it neither sees him nor knows him. You know him, because he abides with you, and he will be in you.

'I will not leave you orphaned; I am coming to you. In a little while the world will no longer see me, but you will see me;

because I live, you also will live. On that day you will know that I am in my Father, and you in me, and I in you. They who have my commandments and keep them are those who love me; and those who love me will be loved by my Father, and I will love them and reveal myself to them.' Judas (not Iscariot) said to him, 'Lord, how is it that you will reveal yourself to us, and not to the world?' Jesus answered him, 'Those who love me will keep my word, and my Father will love them, and we will come to them and make our home with them. Whoever does not love me does not keep my words; and the word that you hear is not mine, but is from the Father who sent me.

I have said these things to you while I am still with you. But the Advocate, the Holy Spirit, whom the Father will send in my name, will teach you everything, and remind you of all that I have said to you.'

In the beginning

As the opening verses of the Old Testament these lines, from Genesis 1:1–5, are among the most familiar in the Bible.

In the beginning God created the heaven and the earth,

And the earth was without form, and void; and darkness was upon the face of the deep. And the Spirit of God moved upon the face of the waters.

And God said, Let there be light: and there was light.

And God saw the light, that it was good: and God divided the light from the darkness.

And God called the light Day, and the darkness he called Night. And the evening and the morning were the first day.

(Authorized [King James] Version)

Invictus

William Ernest Henley was inspired to write his famous poem 'Invictus', a hymn to human endurance, by his ordeal in hospital in Edinburgh in 1873, where he was confined by tubercular arthritis and ultimately had to have a foot amputated. He survived the experience and went on to establish a reputation as a poet and editor, as well as providing the inspiration for Robert Louis Stevenson's character Long John Silver in his novel Treasure Island *(1883).*

Out of the night that covers me,
Black as the pit from pole to pole,
I thank whatever gods may be
For my unconquerable soul.

In the fell clutch of circumstance,
I have not winced nor cried aloud;
Under the bludgeonings of chance
My head is bloody, but unbowed.

Beyond this place of wrath and tears
Looms but the horror of the shade,
And yet the menace of the years
Finds and shall find me unafraid.

It matters not how strait the gate,
How charged with punishments the scroll,
I am the master of my fate;
I am the captain of my soul.

William Ernest Henley (1849–1903)

Jerusalem

Set to music by Sir Hubert Parry, 'Jerusalem' ranks high amongst the most popular of all English hymns. With words from the preface to William Blake's Milton *(1804), the hymn was first performed during a music festival at the Albert Hall and ever since has been a feature of the 'Last Night of the Proms' concert at the same venue.*

Its admirers have included King George V (who wanted Blake's verses adopted as a national anthem), the Labour Party and the Women's Institute, both of which by tradition sing 'Jerusalem' at their meetings.

And did those feet in ancient time
Walk upon England's mountains green?
And was the holy lamb of God
On England's pleasant pastures seen?

And did the Countenance Divine
Shine forth upon our clouded hills?
And was Jerusalem builded here
Among these dark Satanic mills?

Bring me my bow of burning gold!
Bring me my arrows of desire!
Bring me my spear! O clouds, unfold!
Bring me my chariot of fire!

I will not cease from mental fight,
Nor shall my sword sleep in my hand,
Till we have built Jerusalem
In England's green and pleasant land.

William Blake (1757–1827)

Jerusalem the golden

The lines of this hymn come originally from a twelfth-century poem satirizing the corruption of the medieval church and state. The poem was translated into English by J. M. Neale (1818–66) while the music was provided by Lieutenant-Colonel Alexander Ewing (1830–95), apparently the only piece of music this soldier and lawyer ever composed.

Jerusalem the golden,
With milk and honey blest,
Beneath thy contemplation
Sink heart and voice oppressed.
I know not, O I know not
What social joys are there,
What radiancy of glory,
What light beyond compare.

They stand, those halls of Sion,
Conjubilant with song,
And bright with many an angel,
And all the martyr throng:
The Prince is ever in them,
The daylight is serene,
The pastures of the blessed
Are decked in glorious sheen.

There is the throne of David,
And there, from care released,
The song of them that feast;
And they who, with their leader,
Have conquered in the fight,
For ever and ever
Are clad in robes of white.

O sweet and blessed country,
When shall I see thy face?
O sweet and blessed country,
When shall I win thy grace?
Exult, O dust and ashes!
The Lord shall be thy part:
His only, His for ever,
Thou shalt be, and thou art!

Bernard of Cluny (twelfth century)

Jesus Christ is risen today

The words of this hymn were originally written by an unidentified Bohemian author in Latin some time in the fourteenth century and first appeared in English translation in Lyra Davidica *(1708). As a celebration of Christ's resurrection, it is usually sung at Easter.*

Jesus Christ is risen today, Alleluia!
Our triumphant holy day, Alleluia!
Who did once, upon the cross, Alleluia!
Suffer to redeem our loss. Alleluia!

Hymns of praise then let us sing, Alleluia!
Unto Christ, our heavenly King, Alleluia!
Who endured the cross and grave, Alleluia!
Sinners to redeem and save. Alleluia!

For the pains which he endured, Alleluia!
Our salvation have procured; Alleluia!
Now above the sky he's king, Alleluia!
Where the angels ever sing. Alleluia!

Anonymous

Jesus loves me

Anna Bartlett Warner was a novelist and poet who penned these lines for inclusion in her sister Susan's novel Say and Seal *(1859), specifically for a scene in which they are spoken to comfort a dying child. Set to music by William Batchelder Bradbury (1816–68), Anna Warner's poem quickly established itself as a favourite children's hymn.*

Jesus loves me! this I know,
For the Bible tells me so;
Little ones to Him belong,
They are weak but He is strong.

Yes, Jesus loves me!
Yes, Jesus loves me!
Yes, Jesus loves me!
The Bible tells me so.

Jesus loves me! He who died
Heaven's gate to open wide;
He will wash away my sin,
Let His little child come in.

Jesus loves me! He will stay
Close beside me all the way;
Thou hast bled and died for me,
I will henceforth live for Thee.

Anna Bartlett Warner (1820–1915)

Jesus shall reign

Isaac Watts based these verses upon Psalm 72, reapplying praises meant originally for King Solomon to the figure of Christ. Though written long before the launch of the modern missionary movement, Watts' lines subsequently became identified as an impassioned celebration of missionary zeal. This first great missionary hymn has been sung by peoples all round the world, including South Sea Islanders, who sang it at a service celebrating their acceptance of a Christian form of government in 1862.

Jesus shall reign where'er the sun
Does his successive journeys run;
His kingdom stretch from shore to shore,
Till moons shall wax and wane no more.

People and realms of every tongue
Dwell on His love with sweetest song,
And infant voices shall proclaim
Their early blessings on His name.

Blessings abound where'er He reigns;
The prisoner leaps to lose his chains;
The weary find eternal rest,
And all the sons of want are blest.

Let every creature rise and bring
Peculiar honours to our king;
Angels descend with songs again,
And earth repeat the long amen.

Isaac Watts (1674–1748)

Joy to the world

This hymn by Isaac Watts is one of the few that have kept their place in services at Christmas time without being technically a carol (as it does not refer specifically to the birth of Christ). It is based on Psalm 98, which summons the world to celebrate the coming of the Lord.

Joy to the world, the Lord has come!
Let earth receive her King;
Let every heart prepare Him room,
And heaven and nature sing.

Joy to the earth, the Saviour reigns!
Your sweetest songs employ;
While fields and streams and hills and plains
Repeat the sounding joy.

He rules the world with truth and grace,
And makes the nations prove
The glories of His righteousness,
The wonders of His love.

Isaac Watts (1647–1748)

Just as I am

The author of this hymn, Charlotte Elliott, was struck down by illness in her early thirties and spent the rest of her life confined to a wheelchair. She was moved to write these lines after a chastening experience in 1831, frustrated by her inability to help her friends as they prepared a church bazaar and feeling that putting pen to paper was the only way she could contribute. Her lines were inspired in part by John 6:37, which reads 'Him that cometh unto me I will in no wise cast out'. Admirers of the hymn included the poet William Wordsworth, who recited it to his daughter Dora every morning on her deathbed.

Just as I am, without one plea
But that Thy blood was shed for me,
And that Thou bidst me come to Thee,
O Lamb of God, I come.

Just as I am, though tossed about
With many a conflict, many a doubt,
Fightings and fears within, without,
O Lamb of God, I come.

Just as I am, poor, wretched, blind;
Sight, riches, healing of the mind,
Yea all I need, in Thee to find,
O Lamb of God, I come.

Just as I am, Thou wilt receive,
Wilt welcome, pardon, cleanse, relieve:
Because Thy promise I believe,
O Lamb of God, I come.

Just as I am (Thy love unknown
Has broken every barrier down),
Now to be Thine, yea Thine alone,
O Lamb of God, I come.

Just as I am, of that free love
The breadth, length, depth and height to prove,
Here for a season, then above,
O Lamb of God, I come.

Charlotte Elliott (1789–1871)

The King of love my Shepherd is

This hymn, written by Henry Williams Baker, is perhaps the most popular of several versions of Psalm 23 rendered into hymn form over the centuries. Others include George Herbert's 'The God of love my Shepherd is' and 'The Lord's my Shepherd, I'll not want', which was sung at the wedding of Queen Elizabeth and the Duke of Edinburgh and subsequently at countless other marriage services. It is said that Baker himself was heard reciting the third verse of his celebrated creation as he lay on his deathbed at the premature age of 56.

The King of love my Shepherd is,
Whose goodness faileth never;
I nothing lack if I am His,
And He is mine for ever.

Where streams of living water flow
My ransomed soul He leadeth,
And where the verdant pastures grow
With food celestial feedeth.

Perverse and foolish oft I strayed,
But yet in love He sought me,
And on His shoulder gently laid,
And home, rejoicing, brought me.

In death's dark vale I fear no ill
With Thee, dear Lord, beside me;
Thy rod and staff my comfort still,
Thy cross before to guide me.

Thou spread'st a table in my sight,
Thy unction, grace bestoweth;
And O what transport of delight
From Thy pure chalice floweth!

And so through all the length of days
Thy goodness faileth never,
Good Shepherd, may I sing Thy praise
Within Thy house for ever.

Henry Williams Baker (1821–77)

The Lake isle of Innisfree

This poem by Irish poet W. B. Yeats ranks among his most famous works. He composed these lines when reminded by the sound of a fountain playing in a shop-window of the island of Innisfree in Lough Gill, to which as a teenager he had dreamed of retreating in imitation of Henry Thoreau. For many readers Innisfree has variously come to represent a rural idyll or the heaven to which the soul travels after death.

I will arise and go now, and go to Innisfree,
And a small cabin build there, of clay and wattles made:
Nine bean-rows will I have there, a hive for the honey-bee,
And live alone in the bee-loud glade.

And I shall have some peace there, for peace comes dropping
slow,
Dropping from the veils of the morning to where the cricket
sings;
There midnight's all a glimmer, and noon a purple glow,
And evening full of the linnet's wings.

I will arise and go now, for always night and day
I hear lake water lapping with low sounds by the shore;
While I stand on the roadway, or on the pavements grey,
I hear it in the deep heart's core.

W. B. Yeats (1865–1939)

Land of hope and glory

A. C. Benson composed the words of 'Land of hope and glory' for performance at the coronation of Edward VII in 1902. The chorus of his poem was set to a rousing tune by Edward Elgar, that had begun life as 'Pomp and Circumstance March No. 1' (1901) and in due course the resulting song became widely accepted as the unofficial second British national anthem.

For many years it has been part of the climax of the 'Last Night of the Proms' concert, surviving attempts to drop it from the programme in a bid to update the event's traditionalist image.

Dear Land of Hope, thy hope is crowned
God make thee mightier yet!
On Sov'ran brows, belov'd, renown'd,
Once more thy crown is set.
Thine equal laws, by freedom gained,
Have ruled thee well and long;
By Freedom gained, by Truth maintain'd,
Thine Empire shall be strong.

Land of Hope and Glory, Mother of the Free,
How shall we extol thee, who are born of thee?
Wider still and wider shall thy bounds be set,
God, who made thee mighty, make thee mightier yet.
God, who made thee mighty, make thee mightier yet.

Thy fame is ancient as the days,
As Ocean large and wide;
A pride that dares, and heeds not praise,
A stern and silent pride.
Not that false joy that dreams content
With what our sires have won;
The blood a hero sire hath spent
Still nerves a hero son.

Arthur Christopher Benson (1862–1925)

Land of my fathers

The following song was written originally in Welsh under the title 'Hen wlad fy nhadau' and English translations vary. Over the years it has won recognition as the Welsh national anthem, often sung at international rugby matches and on other important occasions.

O land of my fathers, O land of my love,
Dear mother of minstrels who kindle and move,
And hero on hero, who at honour's proud call,
For freedom their lifeblood let fall.

Wales! Wales! O but my heart is with you!
And long as the sea
Your bulwark shall be,
To Cymru my heart shall be true.

O land of the mountains, the bard's paradise,
Whose precipice, valleys lone as the skies,
Green murmuring forest, far echoing flood
Fire the fancy and quicken the blood.

For tho' the fierce foeman has ravaged your realm,
The old speech of Cymru he cannot o'erwhelm,
Our passionate poets to silence command
Or banish the harp from your strand.

Evan Jones (1809–78)

Last lines

Anne Brontë wrote this poem a few weeks after the death of her sister Emily from tuberculosis. By that time Anne knew that she too had contracted the disease and would probably not long survive her sister. According to Charlotte Brontë, 'These lines written, the desk was closed, the pen laid aside – for ever.' The resolute tone of the poem in face of death has made it a lasting favourite.

I hoped, that with the brave and strong,
My portioned task might lie;
To toil amid the busy throng,
With purpose pure and high.

But God has fixed another part,
And He has fixed it well;
I said so with my bleeding heart,
When first the anguish fell.

A dreadful darkness closes in
On my bewildered mind;
Oh, let me suffer and not sin,
Be tortured, yet resigned.

Shall I with joy thy blessings share
And not endure their loss?
Or hope the martyr's crown to wear
And cast away the cross?

Thou, God, hast taken our delight,
Our treasured hope away;
Thou bidst us now weep through the night
And sorrow through the day.

These weary hours will not be lost,
These days of misery,
These nights of darkness, anguish-tost,
Can I but turn to Thee.

Weak and weary though I lie,
Crushed with sorrow, worn with pain,
I may lift to Heaven mine eye,
And strive to labour not in vain;

That inward strife against the sins
That ever wait on suffering
To strike whatever first begins –
Each ill that would corruption bring;

That secret labour to sustain
With humble patience every blow;
To gather fortitude from pain,
And hope and holiness from woe.

Thus let me serve Thee from my heart,
Whate'er may be my written fate:
Whether thus early to depart,
Or yet a while to wait.

If Thou shouldst bring me back to life,
More humbled I should be;
More wise, more strengthened for the strife,
More apt to lean on Thee.

Should death be standing at the gate,
Thus should I keep my vow;
But, Lord! whatever be my fate,
Oh, let me serve Thee now!

Anne Brontë (1820–49)

Lead, kindly light

Cardinal Newman wrote these celebrated lines during a crisis of faith he underwent in 1833, returning to England by ship after falling seriously ill in Sicily. Inspiration came one night when the vessel lay becalmed somewhere between Corsica and Sardinia, Newman spotting a single light shining through the darkness from the distant harbour and seeing in it a symbol of his spiritual need for guidance (he converted to Catholicism some years later). Admirers of Newman's hymn have included Queen Victoria, who had it read to her as she lay on her deathbed.

Lead, kindly light, amid the encircling gloom,
Lead Thou me on;
The night is dark, and I am far from home,
Lead Thou me on.
Keep Thou my feet; I do not ask to see
The distant scene; one step enough for me.

I was not ever thus, nor prayed that Thou
Shouldst lead me on;
I loved to choose and see my path; but now
Lead Thou me on;
I loved the garish day, and, spite of fears,
Pride ruled my will: remember not past years.

So long Thy power hath blest me, sure it still
Will lead me on,
O'er moor and fen, o'er crag and torrent, till
The night is gone;
And with the morn those angel faces smile,
Which I have loved long since, and lost awhile.

Cardinal John Henry Newman (1801–90)

Lead us, heavenly Father, lead us

A popular choice both for weddings and funerals as well as for everyday services, this hymn was the work of James Edmeston, an architect and surveyor who served as churchwarden at a church in east London.

He was in the habit of composing a new hymn to be sung at each weekly Sunday morning service of the London Orphan Asylum: by the time of his death he had contributed in excess of 2000, but this is the only one that has remained popular.

Lead us, heavenly Father, lead us
O'er the world's tempestuous sea;
Guard us, guide us, keep us, feed us,
For we have no help but Thee;
Yet possessing every blessing
If our God our Father be.

Saviour, breathe forgiveness o'er us,
All our weakness Thou dost know;
Thou didst tread this earth before us,
Thou didst feel its keenest woe;
Lone and dreary, faint and weary,
Through the desert Thou didst go.

Spirit of our God descending,
Fill our hearts with heavenly joy;
Love with every passion blending,
Pleasure that can never cloy;
Thus provided, pardoned, guided,
Nothing can our peace destroy.

James Edmeston (1791–1867)

Let the little children come to me

This biblical passage, from Mark 10:13–16, is often quoted as an illustration of Christ's special love for children and of the need for tolerance towards them from adults. It is consequently frequently read at christenings and other services at which children are present.

People were bringing little children to him in order that he might touch them; and the disciples spoke sternly to them. But when Jesus saw this, he was indignant and said to them, 'Let the little children come to me; do not stop them; for it is to such as these that the kingdom of God belongs. Truly I tell you, whoever does not receive the kingdom of God as a little child will never enter it.' And he took them up in his arms, laid his hands on them, and blessed them.

Let us now praise famous men

These lines in honour of past generations come from the biblical Apocrypha, Sirach 44:1–15. Parts of this passage are sometimes quoted in the course of memorial services.

Let us now sing the praises of famous men,
    our ancestors in their generations.
The Lord apportioned to them great glory,
    his majesty from the beginning.
There were those who ruled in their kingdoms,
    and made a name for themselves by their valour;
    those who gave counsel because they were intelligent;
    those who spoke in prophetic oracles;
those who led the people by their counsels
    and by their knowledge of the people's lore;
    they were wise in their words of instruction;
those who composed musical tunes,
    or put verses in writing;
rich men endowed with resources,
    living peacefully in their homes –
all these were honoured in their generations,
    and were the pride of their times.
Some of them have left behind a name,
    so that others declare their praise.
But of others there is no memory;
    they have perished as though they had never existed;
    they have become as though they had never been born,
    they and their children after them.
But these also were godly men,
    whose righteous deeds have not been forgotten;
their wealth will remain with their descendants,
    and their inheritance with their children's children.
Their descendants stand by the covenants;
    their children also, for their sake.
Their offspring will continue for ever,
    and their glory will never be blotted out.

Their bodies are buried in peace,
    but their name lives on generation after generation.
The assembly declares their wisdom,
    and the congregation proclaims their praise.

Let us, with a gladsome mind

This was one of the earliest notable literary productions of the author of the great epic Paradise Lost *and other works. A paraphrase of Psalm 136, it was composed when Milton was a pupil at St Paul's School in London, aged just 15. It was first set to music around 200 years later.*

Let us, with a gladsome mind
Praise the Lord, for He is kind,
For His mercies ay endure,
Ever faithful, ever sure.

Let us blaze His name abroad,
For of gods He is the God:
For His mercies ay endure,
Ever faithful, ever sure.

He with all-commanding might
Filled the new-made world with light:
For His mercies ay endure,
Ever faithful, ever sure.

He the golden-tressed sun
Caused all day his course to run:
For His mercies ay endure,
Ever faithful, ever sure.

And the horned moon by night,
Mid her spangled sisters bright:
For His mercies ay endure,
Ever faithful, ever sure.

All things living He doth feed,
His full hand supplies their need:
For His mercies ay endure,
Ever faithful, ever sure.

Let us, with a gladsome mind,
Praise the Lord, for He is kind:
For His mercies ay endure,
Ever faithful, ever sure.

John Milton (1608–74)

The Listeners

The haunting, enigmatic atmosphere of Walter De la Mare's 'The Listeners' has kept it a popular favourite ever since it was written and it is now perhaps the most anthologized of all his works. There has been much scholarly debate about the identity of the solitary Traveller and the supernatural presence that refuses to respond to his call.

'Is there anybody there?' said the Traveller,
Knocking on the moonlit door;
And his horse in the silence champed the grasses
Of the forest's ferny floor:
And a bird flew up out of the turret,
Above the Traveller's head:
And he smote upon the door again a second time;
'Is there anybody there?' he said.
But no one descended to the Traveller;
No head from the leaf-fringed sill
Leaned over and looked into his grey eyes,
Where he stood perplexed and still.
But only a host of phantom listeners
That dwelt in the lone house then
Stood listening in the quiet of the moonlight
To that voice from the world of men:
Stood thronging the faint moonbeams on the dark stair,
That goes down to the empty hall,
Harkening in an air stirred and shaken
By the lonely Traveller's call.
And he felt in his heart their strangeness,
Their stillness answering his cry,
While his horse moved, cropping the dark turf,
'Neath the starred and leafy sky;
For he suddenly smote on the door, even
Louder, and lifted his head: –
'Tell them I came, and no one answered,
That I kept my word,' he said.
Never the least stir made the listeners,
Though every word he spake
Fell echoing through the shadowiness of the still house
From the one man left awake:

Ay, they heard his foot upon the stirrup,
And the sound of iron on stone,
And how the silence surged softly backward,
When the plunging hoofs were gone.

Walter De La Mare (1873–1956)

The Lord is my shepherd

This prayer appears in the Bible as Psalm 23 and over the centuries has been quoted on innumerable occasions to comfort the dying or to bring reassurance to others in distressing situations.

The LORD is my shepherd, I shall not want.

He maketh me to lie down in green pastures: he leadeth me beside the still waters.

He restoreth my soul: he leadeth me in the paths of righteousness for his name's sake.

Yea, though I walk through the valley of the shadow of death, I will fear no evil: for thou art with me; thy rod and thy staff they comfort me.

Thou preparest a table before me in the presence of mine enemies: thou anointest my head with oil; my cup runneth over.

Surely goodness and mercy shall follow me all the days of my life: and I will dwell in the house of the LORD for ever.

(Authorized [King James] Version)

Lord of all hopefulness

Jan Struther, the author of these lines, is perhaps best known as the creator of Mrs Miniver, the archetypal English country gentlewoman brought to life in a series of articles in The Times *newspaper between the wars. It was upon these articles that the highly successful film* Mrs Miniver *was based. Jan Struther's lines were originally sung to the tune 'Slane', but in 1951 Cyril Taylor contributed an alternative tune that he called 'Miniver' after the author's famous character.*

Lord of all hopefulness, Lord of all joy,
Whose trust, ever child-like, no cares could destroy,
Be there at our waking, and give us, we pray,
Your bliss in our hearts, Lord, at the break of the day.

Lord of all eagerness, Lord of all faith,
Whose strong hands were skilled at the plane and the lathe,
Be there at our labours, and give us, we pray,
Your strength in our hearts, Lord, at the noon of the day.

Lord of all kindliness, Lord of all grace,
Your hands swift to welcome, your arms to embrace,
Be there at our homing, and give us, we pray,
Your love in our hearts, Lord, at the eve of the day.

Lord of all gentleness, Lord of all calm,
Whose voice is contentment, whose presence is balm,
Be there at our sleeping, and give us, we pray,
Your peace in our hearts, Lord, at the end of the day.

Jan Struther (Joyce Placzek; 1901–53)

The Lord's Prayer

The words for the Lord's Prayer are spoken by Christ at Matthew 6:9-13. The prayer comes in Christ's Sermon on the Mount and is a model as to how we should pray to God our Father, that he should be considered holy, that his rule should come more and more fully, that our needs may be met each day, our sins forgiven and that we will be kept faithful to him in times of difficulty.

Our Father which art in heaven, Hallowed be thy name.

Thy kingdom come. Thy will be done in earth, as it is in heaven.

Give us this day our daily bread.

And forgive us our debts, as we forgive our debtors.

And lead us not into temptation, but deliver us from evil:

For thine is the kingdom, and the power, and the glory, for ever. Amen.

(Authorized [King James] Version)

Loud is the vale

William Wordsworth wrote these lines in 1806 in tribute to the dying English politician Charles James Fox. At the time of his death Fox was on the point of introducing a bill abolishing the slave trade. The poem is sometimes recited in honour of great statesmen and others.

Loud is the vale; this inland depth
In peace is roaring like the sea;
Yon star upon the mountain-top
Is listening quietly.

A power is passing from the earth
To breathless Nature's dark abyss;
But when the mighty pass away
What is it more than this,

That man who is from God sent forth
Doth yet again to God return?
Such ebb and flow must ever be,
Then wherefore should we mourn?

William Wordsworth (1770–1850)

Love alters not

William Shakespeare's 'Sonnet 116' is a hymn to the constancy of true love. It is consequently an occasional choice of reading at wedding celebrations.

Let me not to the marriage of true minds
Admit impediments; love is not love
Which alters when it alteration finds,
Or bends with the remover to remove.
O, no, it is an ever-fixèd mark
That looks on tempests and is never shaken;
It is the star to every wand'ring bark,
Whose worth's unknown, although his height be taken.
Love's not Time's fool, though rosy lips and cheeks,
Within his bending sickle's compass come;
Love alters not with his brief hours and weeks,
But bears it out even to the edge of doom.
  If this be error and upon me proved,
  I never writ, nor no man ever loved.

William Shakespeare (1564–1616)

Love divine, all loves excelling

One of the most popular in the prodigious output of the Methodist hymn writer Charles Wesley, this is a particular favourite for weddings. It was inspired by 'The Song of Venus' from John Dryden's play King Arthur, *which started with the line 'Fairest isle, all isles excelling'. The original song was set to music by Henry Purcell, but today the hymn is variously sung either to Purcell's tune, to another by John Stainer, to 'Blaenwern' by the Welsh composer William Penfro Rowlands, or to 'Hyfrydol' by Rowland Huw Pritchard.*

Love divine, all loves excelling,
Joy of heaven to earth come down,
Fix in us Thy humble dwelling,
All Thy faithful mercies crown.
Jesu, Thou art all compassion,
Pure, unbounded love Thou art;
Visit us with Thy salvation,
Enter every trembling heart.

Come, almighty to deliver,
Let us all Thy life receive;
Suddenly return, and never,
Never more Thy temples leave.
Thee we would be always blessing,
Serve Thee as Thy hosts above,
Pray, and praise Thee, without ceasing,
Glory in Thy perfect love.

Finish then Thy new creation,
Pure and sinless let us be;
Let us see Thy great salvation,
Perfectly restored in Thee;
Changed from glory into glory,
Till in heaven we take our place,
Till we cast our crowns before Thee,
Lost in wonder, love and praise.

Charles Wesley (1707–88)

Love lives beyond the tomb

Many of the most famous poems of English ploughman-poet John Clare dwell upon the themes of love and loss. Clare himself was mentally unstable throughout his life and never really escaped the distress he suffered as a young man when he parted company with his first love, Mary Joyce. In 1841 he escaped from the asylum at High Beach, Epping and walked all the way home to Northamptonshire under the delusion that he was married to Mary and would be happily reunited with her.

Love lives beyond
The tomb, the earth, which fades like dew.
I love the fond,
The faithful, and the true.

Love lives in sleep,
The happiness of healthy dreams
Eve's dews may weep,
But love delightful seems.

'Tis heard in Spring
When light and sunbeams, warm and kind,
On angels' wing
Bring love and music to the mind.

And where is voice,
So young, so beautiful and sweet
As nature's choice,
Where Spring and lovers meet?

Love lives beyond
The tomb, the earth, the flowers, and dew.
I love the fond,
The faithful, young and true.

John Clare (1793–1864)

Love seeketh not itself to please

William Blake's 'The Clod and the Pebble' is one of his best-loved works. Contrasting opposing optimistic and pessimistic views of love, it illuminates the dual nature of love, which can both ease the heart and break it.

"Love seeketh not Itself to please,
Nor for itself hath any care,
But for another gives its ease,
And builds a Heaven in Hell's despair."
So sang little Clod of Clay
Trodden with the cattle's feet.

But a Pebble of the brook
Warbled out these metres meet:
"Love seeketh only Self to please,
To bind another to Its delight,
Joys in another's loss of ease,
And builds a Hell in Heaven's despite."

William Blake (1757–1827)

Make me a channel of your peace

When John Temple, a South African-born Roman Catholic hymn writer, was asked to provide some new songs for the Franciscans in Los Angeles, he turned to a prayer traditionally attributed to St Francis of Assisi (1182–1226) and produced the following lines. In fact, it would appear that St Francis probably was not the author of the original prayer, which may have been the work of the Franciscan Jacopo di Toddi.

Make me a channel of your peace
Where there is hatred let me bring your love;
Where there is injury, your pardon, LORD:
And where there's doubt, true faith in you.

Oh, Master, grant that I may never seek
So much to be consoled as to console;
To be understood as to understand,
To be loved, as to love with all my soul.

Make me a channel of your peace.
Where there's despair in life, let me bring hope;
Where there is darkness only light;
And where there's sadness, ever joy.

Make me a channel of your peace.
It is in pardoning that we are pardoned,
In giving to all men that we receive;
And in dying that we're born to eternal life.

John Sebastian Temple (Johann Sebastian von Tempelhoff; b.1928)

Many waters cannot quench love

The Song of Solomon is often singled out as the most poetic book of the Bible. These verses, found at 8:6-14, celebrate the conquering power of love and selected lines from them are consequently much quoted.

Set me as a seal upon your heart,
    as a seal upon your arm; for love is strong as death,
    passion fierce as the grave.
    Its flashes are flashes of fire,
    a raging flame.
Many waters cannot quench love,
    neither can floods drown it.
    If one offered for love
    all the wealth of one's house,
    it would be utterly scorned.
We have a little sister,
    and she has no breasts.
    What shall we do for our sister,
    on the day when she is spoken for?
If she is a wall,
    we will build upon her a battlement of silver;
    but if she is a door,
    we will enclose her with boards of cedar.
I was a wall,
    and my breasts were like towers;
    then I was in his eyes
    as one who brings peace.
Solomon had a vineyard at Baal-hamon;
    he entrusted the vineyard to keepers;
    each one was to bring for its fruit a thousand pieces of
    silver.
My vineyard, my very own, is for myself;
    you, O Solomon, may have the thousand,
    and the keepers of the fruit two hundred!
O you who dwell in the gardens,
    my companions are listening for your voice;
    let me hear it.

Make haste, my beloved,
    and be like a gazelle
or a young stag
    upon the mountains of spices!

May the road rise to meet you

This heartfelt Irish blessing by an unknown author is sometimes quoted as an expression of good wishes at times of parting.

May the road rise to meet you,
May the wind be always at your back.
May the sun shine warm upon your face,
The rains fall soft upon your fields.

And until we meet again,
May God hold you in the palm of his hand.
May God be with you and bless you;
May you see your children's children.

May you be poor in misfortune,
Rich in blessings,
May you know nothing but happiness
From this day forward.

May the road rise to meet you,
May the wind be always at your back.
May the warm rays of sun fall upon your home
And may the hand of a friend always be near.

May green be the grass you walk on,
May blue be the skies above you,
May pure be the joys that surround you,
May true be the hearts that love you.

Anonymous

Mine eyes have seen the glory of the coming of the Lord

Julia Ward Howe wrote these lines in 1861 during the American Civil War, inspired by hearing soldiers singing the rousing abolitionist song 'John Brown's body', the tune of which she borrowed for her own verses. In so doing she was (probably unwittingly) returning the song to its original context, as it had begun life some time during the 1850s in the form of a Methodist hymn entitled 'Say, brother, will you meet us'. Formally called the 'Battle Hymn of the American Republic', Howe's adaptation became a popular marching song of the Federal forces and it has since acquired the status of a national song in the USA, being sung at all manner of public events, from parades to presidential inaugurations.

Mine eyes have seen the glory of the coming of the Lord;
He is trampling out the vintage where the grapes of wrath are stored;
He hath loosed the fateful lightning of His terrible swift sword:
His truth is marching on.

I have seen Him in the watch-fires of a hundred circling camps;
They have builded Him an altar in the evening dews and damps;
I can read His righteous sentence by the dim and flaring lamps:
His day is marching on.

I have read a fiery gospel, writ in burnished rows of steel:
'As you deal with my contemners, so with you my grace shall deal;'
Let the hero born of woman crush the serpent with His heel,
Since God is marching on.

He hath sounded forth the trumpet that shall never call retreat;
He is sifting out the hearts of men before his judgment-seat:
Oh, be swift, my soul, to answer Him; be jubilant, my feet!
Our God is marching on.

In the beauty of the lilies Christ was born across the sea,
With a glory in His bosom that transfigures you and me;
As He died to make men holy, let us die to make men free,
While God is marching on.

He is coming like the glory of the morning on the wave;
He is wisdom to the mighty, He is succour to the brave;
So the world shall be His footstool, and the soul of time His
slave;
Our God is marching on.

Julia Ward Howe (1819–1910)

Miss me – but let me go

This poem, by an unknown author, is regularly heard at funeral services. It offers both consolation to the bereaved concerning the person they have lost and encouragement to them to return to their own lives.

When I come to the end of the road
And the sun has set for me
I want no rites in a gloom-filled room
Why cry for a soul set free?

Miss me a little, but not too long
And not with your head bowed low
Remember the love that we once shared
Miss me but let me go.

For this is a journey that we all must take
And each must go alone
It's all a part of life's plan
A step on the road to home.

When you are lonely and sick at heart
Go to the friends we know
And bury your sorrows in doing good deeds
Miss me but let me go.

Anonymous

Morning has broken

The children's writer Eleanor Farjeon contributed the following lines for a new hymnal published in 1931 and it soon became a popular favourite. It enjoyed a new lease of life in the early 1970s when it was recorded by the pop singer Cat Stevens and entered the Top Ten in the pop charts on both sides of the Atlantic.

Farjeon went on to explore the possibilities of spiritualism and reincarnation before ultimately converting to Roman Catholicism, while Stevens responded to the call of religion by converting to Islam.

Morning has broken
Like the first morning,
Blackbird has spoken
Like the first bird.
Praise for the singing,
Praise for the morning,
Praise for them, springing
Fresh from the Word!

Sweet the rain's new fall
Sunlit from heaven,
Like the first dewfall
On the first grass.
Praise for the sweetness
Of the wet garden,
Sprung in completeness
Where His feet pass.

Mine is the sunlight;
Mine is the morning,
Born of the one light
Eden saw play!
Praise with elation,
Praise every morning,
God's re-creation
Of the new day!

Eleanor Farjeon (1881–1965)

My God, how wonderful Thou art

The Yorkshire-born Frederick William Faber belonged to the Anglican Church before converting to Roman Catholicism in 1845, at the age of 31. His new church, however, he felt lacked the richness of hymns available to Protestants and he determined to improve the situation by writing his own hymns, eventually contributing around 150 in all.

My God, how wonderful Thou art,
Thy majesty how bright,
How beautiful Thy mercy-seat,
In depths of burning light!

How dread are Thine eternal years,
O everlasting Lord,
By prostrate spirits day and night
Incessantly adored!

How wonderful, how beautiful,
The sight of Thee must be,
Thine endless wisdom, boundless power,
And awesome purity!

O, how I fear Thee, living God,
With deepest, tenderest fears,
And worship Thee with trembling hope,
And penitential tears!

Yet I may love Thee too, O Lord,
Almighty as Thou art,
For Thou hast stooped to ask of me
The love of my poor heart.

No earthly father loves like Thee,
No mother, e'er so mild,
Bears and forbears as Thou has done
With me Thy sinful child.

Father of Jesus, love's reward,
What rapture will it be
Prostrate before Thy throne to lie,
And gaze and gaze on Thee!
Frederick William Faber (1814–63)

My song is love unknown

The Anglican clergyman Samuel Crossman wrote these lines in the seventeenth century, but it was not until composer John Ireland was asked to contribute a new setting for them, largely replacing the original tune 'Christchurch', that this hymn became a universal favourite and a popular choice for weddings. The story goes that Ireland composed his much-loved music for the hymn in just 15 minutes, writing on a scrap of paper.

My song is love unknown,
My Saviour's love to me,
Love to the loveless shown,
That they might lovely be.
O, who am I,
That for my sake
My Lord should take
Frail flesh, and die?

He came from His blest throne,
Salvation to bestow:
But men made strange, and none
The longed-for Christ would know.
But O, my friend,
My friend indeed,
Who at my need
His life did spend!

Sometimes they strew His way,
And His sweet praises sing;
Resounding all the day
Hosannas to their King.
Then 'Crucify!'
Is all their breath,
And for His death
They thirst and cry.

Why, what hath my Lord done?
What makes this rage and spite?
He made the lame to run,
He gave the blind their sight.
Sweet injuries!
Yet they at these
Themselves displease,
And 'gainst Him rise.

They rise, and needs will have
My dear Lord made away;
A murderer they save,
The Prince of Life they slay.
Yet cheerful He
To suffering goes,
That He His foes
From thence might free.

In life no house, no home,
My Lord on earth might have;
In death no friendly tomb,
But what a stranger gave.
What may I say?
Heaven was His home;
But mine the tomb
Wherein He lay.

Here might I stay and sing,
No story so divine;
Never was love, dear King,
Never was grief like Thine!
This is my friend,
In whose sweet praise
I all my days
Could gladly spend.

Samuel Crossman (1624–83)

Nearer, my God, to thee

Sarah Adams wrote this hymn in response to a request from a local clergyman, who needed a hymn to accompany a sermon he was planning on the subject of Jacob's ladder. Adams herself had turned to hymn writing after many setbacks in life, including the death of her mother while she was still a child and enforced retirement from her career as a stage actress at the age of 32 due to ill health. Her hymn is uniquely associated with the Titanic disaster of 1912 and the possibly apocryphal story that this was the tune the band struck up as the stricken liner made its final plunge beneath the waves.

Nearer, my God, to Thee,
Nearer to Thee!
E'en though it be a cross
That raiseth me,
Still all my song shall be,
'Nearer, my God, to Thee,
Nearer to Thee!'

Though, like the wanderer,
The sun gone down,
Darkness be over me,
My rest a stone,
Yet in my dreams I'd be
Nearer, my God, to Thee,
Nearer to Thee!

There let the way appear,
Steps unto heaven;
All that Thou sendest me
In mercy given:
Angels to beckon me
Nearer, my God, to Thee,
Nearer to Thee!

Then, with my waking thoughts
Bright with Thy praise,
Out of my stony griefs
Bethel I'll raise;
So by my woes to be
Nearer, my God, to Thee,
Nearer to Thee!

Or if on joyful wing
Cleaving the sky,
Sun, moon, and stars forgot,
Upwards I fly,
Still all my song shall be,
'Nearer, my God, to Thee,
Nearer to Thee!'

Sarah Flower Adams (1805–48)

A new heaven and a new earth

In these verses, from Revelation 21:1–5 and 22:13–20, which come at the very end of the New Testament, St John describes the new Jerusalem, the church of Christ in heaven.

Then I saw a new heaven and a new earth; for the first heaven and the first earth had passed away, and the sea was no more. And I saw the holy city, the new Jerusalem, coming down out of heaven from God, prepared as a bride adorned for her husband. And I heard a loud voice from the throne saying,

'See, the home of God is among mortals.
He will dwell with them; they will be his peoples,
and God himself will be with them;
he will wipe every tear from their eyes.
Death will be no more;
mourning and crying and pain will be no more,
for the first things have passed away.'

And the one who was seated on the throne said, 'See, I am making all things new.' Also he said, 'Write this, for these words are trustworthy and true.'

'I am the Alpha and the Omega, the first and the last, the beginning and the end.'

Blessed are those who wash their robes, so that they will have the right to the tree of life and may enter the city by the gates. Outside are the dogs and sorcerers and fornicators and murderers and idolaters, and everyone who loves and practises falsehood.

'It is I, Jesus, who sent my angel to you with this testimony for the churches. I am the root and the descendant of David, the bright morning star.'

The Spirit and the bride say, 'Come.'
And let everyone who hears say, 'Come.'
And let everyone who is thirsty come.
Let anyone who wishes take the water of life as a gift.

I warn everyone who hears the words of the prophecy of this book: if anyone adds to them, God will add to that person the plagues described in this book; if anyone takes away from the words of the book of this prophecy, God will take away that person's share in the tree of life and in the holy city, which are described in this book.

The one who testifies to these things says, 'Surely I am coming soon.'

Amen. Come, LORD Jesus!

No coward soul is mine

This poem was the last one composed by Emily Brontë before her premature death from tuberculosis. The author's spirited refutation of death in these lines has made the poem an occasional choice of reading at funerals.

No coward soul is mine,
No trembler in the world's storm-troubled sphere:
I see Heaven's glories shine,
And faith shines equal, arming me from fear.

O God within my breast,
Almighty, ever-present Deity!
Life – that in me has rest,
As I – undying Life – have power in Thee!

Vain are the thousand creeds
That move men's hearts; unutterably vain;
Worthless as withered weeds,
Or idlest froth amid the boundless main.

To waken doubt in one
Holding so fast by Thine infinity;
So surely anchored on
The steadfast rock of immortality.

With wide-embracing love
Thy spirit animates eternal years,
Pervades and broods above,
Changes, sustains, dissolves, creates, and rears.

Though earth and man were gone,
And suns and universes ceased to be,
And Thou were left alone,
Every existence would exist in Thee.

There is not room for Death,
Nor atom that his might could render void;
Thou – Thou art Being and Breath,
And what Thou art may never be destroyed.

Emily Brontë (1818–48)

No man is an island

As well as being revered as a poet, John Donne was also noted as a preacher and wrote extensively upon such topics as death and resurrection. This passage, from Devotions upon Emergent Occasions, *is perhaps the most famous of his meditations upon mortality.*

Now, this bell tolling softly for another, says to me: Thou must die.

Perchance he for whom this bell tolls may be so ill, as that he knows not it tolls for him; and perchance I may think myself so much better than I am, as that they who are about me, and see my state, may have caused it to toll for me, and I know not that. The church is Catholic, universal, so are all her actions; all that she does belongs to all. When she baptizes a child, that action concerns me; for that child is thereby connected to that body which is my head too, and ingrafted into that body whereof I am a member. And when she buries a man, that action concerns me: all mankind is of one author, and is one volume; when one man dies, one chapter is not torn out of the book, but translated into a better language; and every chapter must be so translated; God employs several translators; some pieces are translated by age, some by sickness, some by war, some by justice; but God's hand is in every translation, and his hand shall bind up all our scattered leaves again for that library where every book shall lie open to one another. As therefore the bell that rings to a sermon calls not upon the preacher only, but upon the congregation to come, so this bell calls us all; but how much more me, who am brought so near the door by this sickness. There was a contention as far as a suit (in which both piety and dignity, religion and estimation, were mingled), which of the religious orders should ring to prayers first in the morning; and it was determined, that they should ring first that rose earliest. If we understand aright the dignity of this bell that tolls for our evening prayer, we would be glad to make it ours by rising early, in that application, that it might be ours as well as his, whose indeed it is. The bell doth toll for him that thinks it doth; and though it intermit again, yet from that minute that that occasion wrought upon him, he is united to God. Who casts not up his eye to the sun when it rises? but who takes off his eye from a comet when that breaks out? Who bends not his ear to any bell which upon any occasion rings? but who can remove it from that bell which is passing a piece of himself out of this world?

No man is an island, entire of itself; every man is a piece of the continent, a part of the main. If a clod be washed away by the sea, Europe is the less, as well as if a promontory were, as well as if a manor of thy friend's or of thine own were: any man's death diminishes me, because I am involved in mankind, and therefore never send to know for whom the bell tolls; it tolls for thee. Neither can we call this a begging of misery, or a borrowing of misery, as though we were not miserable enough of ourselves, but must fetch in more from the next house, in taking upon us the misery of our neighbours. Truly it were an excusable covetousness if we did, for affliction is a treasure, and scarce any man hath enough of it. No man hath affliction enough that is not matured and ripened by and made fit for God by that affliction. If a man carry treasure in bullion, or in a wedge of gold, and have none coined into current money, his treasure will not defray him as he travels. Tribulation is treasure in the nature of it, but it is not current money in the use of it, except we get nearer and nearer our home, heaven, by it. Another man may be sick too, and sick to death, and this affliction may lie in his bowels, as gold in a mine, and be of no use to him; but this bell, that tells me of his affliction, digs out and applies that gold to me: if by this consideration of another's danger I take mine own into contemplation, and so secure myself, by making my recourse to my God, who is our only security.

John Donne (c.1572–1631)

No room at the inn

This passage detailing the circumstances of Christ's birth, as related at Luke 2:1-7, is one of the readings delivered every year during the Christmas period throughout the Christian world. The phrase 'no room at the inn' has long since entered the language.

In those days a decree went out from Emperor Augustus that all the world should be registered. This was the first registration and was taken while Quirinius was governor of Syria. All went to their own towns to be registered. Joseph also went from the town of Nazareth in Galilee to Judea, to the city of David called Bethlehem, because he was descended from the house and family of David. He went to be registered with Mary, to whom he was engaged and who was expecting a child. While they were there, the time came for her to deliver her child. And she gave birth to her firstborn son and wrapped him in bands of cloth, and laid him in a manger, because there was no place for them in the inn.

No single thing abides

This passage, from Book III of On the Nature of Things *by the Roman writer Lucretius, writing in the first century* BC, *discusses the temporary nature of things. It is occasionally quoted at funerals.*

No single thing abides; but all things flow.
Fragment to fragment clings the things thus grow
Until we name and name them. By degrees they
Melt, and are not more the things we know.
Globed from the atoms falling slow or swift
I see the suns, I see the systems lift their forms;
And even the systems and the suns
Shall go back slowly to the eternal drift.
Thou too, oh earth thine empires, lands and seas
Least with thy stars of all the galaxies.
Globed from the drift like these thou too shalt go.
Thou art going, hour by hour, like these.
Nothing abides.
Thy seas in delicate haze go off;
Those mooned sands forsake their place
And were they are, all other seas in turn
Mow with their scythes of whiteness other bays…
The seeds that once were we take and fly,
Winnowed to earth or whirled along the sky.
Not lost but disunited. Life lives on.
It is the lives, the lives, the lives that die.

Lucretius (Titus Lucretius Carus; c.99–55 BC*)*

The noblest Roman of them all

Mark Antony's lament for Brutus in William Shakespeare's Julius Caesar (1599) is sometimes quoted, in full or in part, in epitaphs and in the course of funeral services.

This was the noblest Roman of them all:
All the conspirators save only he
Did that they did in envy of great Caesar;
He only, in a general honest thought
And common good to all, made one of them.
His life was gentle, and the elements
So mixed in him that Nature might stand up
And say to all the world, 'This was a man!'

William Shakespeare (1564–1616)

Now thank we all our God

Such is the popularity of this hymn in its author Martin Rinkart's native land that is often referred to as the 'German Te Deum'. Rinkart was the Lutheran archdeacon of the town of Eilenburg in Saxony during the Thirty Years' War (1616–48) and he wrote this hymn at a time of great suffering for his flock. Not only had the town been sacked by the Austrians and the Swedes in turn, but it had also been badly affected by plague and then famine. The dead included Rinkart's own wife. Rinkart's hymn was sung at the thanksgiving services that greeted the signing of the Peace of Westphalia in 1648; today it is a popular choice for weddings and other joyful occasions.

Now thank we all our God,
With heart and hands and voices,
Who wondrous things hath done,
In whom His world rejoices;
Who from our mothers' arms
Hath blessed us on our way
With countless gifts of love,
And still is ours today.

O may this bounteous God
Through all our life be near us,
With ever joyful hearts
And blessed peace to cheer us;
And keep us in His grace,
And guide us when perplexed,
And free us from all ills
In this world and the next.

All praise and thanks to God
The Father now be given,
The Son, and Him who reigns
With them in highest heaven,
The one eternal God,
Whom heaven and earth adore;
For thus it was, is now,
And shall be evermore.

Martin Rinkart (1586–1649)

O captain! my captain!

Walt Whitman was inspired to write these lines by the assassination of US President Abraham Lincoln in 1865. Today the poem still expresses the universal sense of loss felt by society as a whole when a great leader or other public figure is lost.

O Captain! my Captain! Our fearful trip is done;
The ship has weathered every rack,
The prize we sought is won;
The port is near, the bells I hear,
The people all exulting,
While follow eyes the steady keel,
The vessel grim and daring;
  But O heart! heart! heart!
  O the bleeding drops of red,
  Where on the deck my Captain lies,
  Fallen cold and dead.

O Captain! my Captain! Rise up and hear the bells;
Rise up – for you the flag is flung,
For you the bugle trills:
For you bouquets and ribboned wreaths,
For you the shores a-crowding;
For you they call, the swaying mass,
Their eager faces turning;
  Here, Captain! dear father!
  This arm beneath your head;
  It is some dream that on the deck
  You've fallen cold and dead.

My Captain does not answer, his lips are pale and still;
My father does not feel my arm,
He has no pulse nor will,
The ship is anchored safe and sound,
Its voyage closed and done;
From fearful trip, the victor ship
Comes in with object won:
    Exult, O shores, and ring, O bells!
    But I, with mournful tread,
    Walk the deck my Captain lies,
    Fallen cold and dead.

Walt Whitman (1819–92)

O come, all ye faithful

This familiar Christmas carol only became widely known after following a somewhat circuitous route. John Francis Wade was a copier of manuscripts who penned these verses in Latin and then included them in a packet of manuscripts sent to the English Roman Catholic College in Lisbon in 1750. It was not until 1785 that they found their way back to England and, via the Portuguese chapel in London, began the process of becoming a worldwide favourite.

O come, all ye faithful,
Joyful and triumphant,
O come ye, O come ye to Bethlehem:
Come and behold Him
Born the King of angels:

O come, let us adore Him,
O come, let us adore Him,
O come, let us adore Him,
Christ the Lord!

God of God,
Light of light,
Lo, He abhors not the virgin's womb;
Very God,
Begotten, not created:

See how the shepherds,
Summoned to His cradle,
Leaving their flocks, draw nigh with lowly fear;
We too will thither
Bend our joyful footsteps:

Lo, star-led chieftains,
Magi, Christ adoring,
Offer Him incense, gold and myrrh;
We to the Christ-child
Bring our hearts' oblations:

Sing, choirs of angels,
Sing in exultation,
Sing, all ye citizens of heaven above,
'Glory to God
In the highest':

Yea, Lord, we greet Thee,
Born this happy morning,
Jesu, to Thee be all glory given;
Word of the Father,
Now in flesh appearing:

John Francis Wade (c.1711–86)

O come, O come, Emmanuel

The work of an unidentified German hymn writer of the early eighteenth century, subsequently translated into English by John Mason Neale (1818–66), this hymn has its origins in the antiphons sung each day during Advent as far back as the ninth century. These antiphons comprised brief verses celebrating the coming of Christ, each beginning with 'O' – and were thus known as the 'Great O's of Advent'. The high-ranking monks of medieval monasteries were allotted one antiphon each and were expected to 'pay' for this privilege by providing hospitality for all present on the day that they sang their verse. The modern hymn resulted from these antiphons being strung together.

O come, O come, Emmanuel,
And ransom captive Israel,
That mourns in lonely exile here
Until the Son of God appear:

Rejoice! Rejoice! Emmanuel
Shall come to thee, O Israel.

O come, thou Wisdom from above
Who orderest all things through Thy love;
To us the path of knowledge show
And teach us in her ways to go:

O come, O come, thou Lord of might,
Who to Thy tribes, on Sinai's height,
In ancient times didst give the law
In cloud, and majesty, and awe:

O come, thou Rod of Jesse, free
Thine own from Satan's tyranny;
From depths of hell Thy people save,
And give them victory o'er the grave:

O come, thou Key of David, come
And open wide our heavenly home;
Make safe the way that leads on high,
And close the path to misery:

O come, thou Dayspring, come and cheer
Our spirits by Thine advent here;
Disperse the gloomy clouds of night,
And death's dark shadows put to flight:

O come, Desire of nations, bring
All peoples to their Saviour King;
Thou Corner-stone, who makest one,
Complete in us Thy work begun:

Anonymous

O death, where is thy sting?

This passage, from 1 Corinthians 15:41–58, records Paul's words concerning the resurrection of the dead. It is consequently sometimes quoted in the course of funeral services.

There is one glory of the sun, and another glory of the moon, and another glory of the stars; indeed, star differs from star in glory.

So it is with the resurrection of the dead. What is sown is perishable, what is raised is imperishable. It is sown in dishonour, it is raised in glory. It is sown in weakness, it is raised in power. It is sown a physical body, it is raised a spiritual body. If there is a physical body, there is also a spiritual body. Thus it is written, 'The first man, Adam, became a living being'; the last Adam became a life-giving spirit. But it is not the spiritual that is first, but the physical, and then the spiritual. The first man was from the earth, a man of dust; the second man is from heaven. As was the man of dust, so are those who are of the dust; and as is the man of heaven, so are those who are of heaven. Just as we have borne the image of the man of dust, we will also bear the image of the man of heaven.

What I am saying, brothers and sisters, is this: flesh and blood cannot inherit the kingdom of God, nor does the perishable inherit the imperishable. Listen, I will tell you a mystery! We will not all die, but we will all be changed, in a moment, in the twinkling of an eye, at the last trumpet. For the trumpet will sound, and the dead will be raised imperishable, and we will be changed. For this perishable body must put on imperishability, and this mortal body must put on immortality. When this perishable body puts on imperishability, and this mortal body puts on immortality, then the saying that is written will be fulfilled:

'Death has been swallowed up in victory.'

'Where, O death, is your victory?
Where, O death, is your sting?'

The sting of death is sin, and the power of sin is the law. But thanks be to God, who gives us the victory through our Lord Jesus Christ.

Therefore, my beloved, be steadfast, immovable, always excelling in the work of the LORD, because you know that in the Lord your labour is not in vain.

O for a closer walk with God

William Cowper penned these verses on 9 December 1769 during a rare respite from his mental agonies. At the time he was particularly concerned about the serious illness of his housekeeper Mrs Unwin, without whom he felt he would be utterly unable to cope with life. It was published as one of the Olney Hymns *in 1779.*

O for a closer walk with God,
A calm and heavenly frame;
A light to shine upon the road
That leads me to the Lamb!

Where is the blessedness I knew
When first I saw the Lord?
Where is the soul-refreshing view
Of Jesus and His word?

What peaceful hours I once enjoyed,
How sweet their memory still!
But they have left an aching void
The world can never fill.

Return, O holy Dove, return,
Sweet messenger of rest;
I hate the sins that made Thee mourn,
And drove Thee from my breast.

The dearest idol I have known,
Whate'er that idol be,
Help me to tear it from Thy throne,
And worship only Thee.

So shall my walk be close with God,
Calm and serene my frame;
So purer light shall mark the road
That leads me to the Lamb.

William Cowper (1731–1800)

O for a heart to praise my God

This hymn was written by Charles Wesley some four years after his conversion. It took as its starting point Psalm 51:10, which runs 'Create in me a pure heart, O God.'

O for a heart to praise my God,
A heart from sin set free;
A heart that always feels Thy blood
So freely spilt for me:

A heart resigned, submissive, meek,
My dear Redeemer's throne,
Where only Christ is heard to speak,
Where Jesus reigns alone:

A humble, lowly, contrite heart,
Believing, true, and clean;
Which neither life nor death can part
From Him that dwells within:

A heart in every thought renewed,
And filled with love divine;
Perfect, and right, and pure, and good,
A copy, Lord, of Thine!

Thy nature, gracious Lord, impart,
Come quickly from above,
Write Thy new name upon my heart,
Thy new best name of love.

Charles Wesley (1707–88)

O for a thousand tongues to sing

Charles Wesley composed these verses on 21 May 1749 to celebrate the anniversary of his conversion on 21 May 1738 and they were originally entitled 'For the Anniversary Day of One's Conversion'. The opening line was a quotation from the Moravian leader Peter Bohler, by whom both Charles Wesley and his brother John were profoundly influenced: 'Had I a thousand tongues, I would praise Christ Jesus with all of them.'

O for a thousand tongues to sing
My dear Redeemer's praise,
The glories of my God and King,
The triumphs of His grace!

Jesus – the name that charms our fears,
That bids our sorrows cease;
'Tis music in the sinner's ears,
'Tis life, and health, and peace.

He breaks the power of cancelled sin,
He sets the prisoner free;
His blood can make the foulest clean,
His blood availed for me.

He speaks; and, listening to His voice,
New life the dead receive;
The mournful, broken hearts rejoice;
The humble poor believe.

Hear him, ye deaf; His praise, ye dumb,
Your loosened tongues employ;
Ye blind, behold your Saviour come;
And leap, ye lame, for joy!

See all your sins on Jesus laid:
The Lamb of God was slain;
His soul was once an offering made
For every soul of man.

In Christ, our Head, you then shall know,
Shall feel, your sins forgiven,
Anticipate your heaven below,
And own that love is heaven.

My gracious master and my God,
Assist me to proclaim,
To spread through all the earth abroad
The honours of Thy name.

Charles Wesley (1707–88)

O God, our help in ages past

This hymn was penned by Isaac Watts in 1714 at a time of considerable national distress: Queen Anne lay dying and, with no obvious heir, it was uncertain what fate lay in store for those who might have offended any new ruler, especially those who belonged to religious minorities. Watts' own father had been imprisoned for his religious views; hence, the impulse of Isaac Watts to turn to Psalm 90 for comfort. Today it is often sung at Remembrance Day services and on other solemn occasions.

O God, our help in ages past,
Our hope for years to come,
Our shelter from the stormy blast
And our eternal home!

Before the hills in order stood,
Or Earth received her frame,
From everlasting Thou art God,
To endless years the same.

A thousand ages in Thy sight
Are like an evening gone;
Short as the watch that ends the night
Before the rising Sun.

Time, like an ever-rolling stream,
Bears all its sons away;
They fly, forgotten, as a dream
Dies at the opening day.

O God, our help in ages past,
Our hope for years to come,
Be Thou our guard while troubles last
And our eternal home.

Isaac Watts (1674–1748)

O Jesus, I have promised

A scholar and rector of Castle Camps in Cambridgeshire, John Bode had two sons and one daughter, who were presented for confirmation together in 1866. To mark the occasion the proud father felt the need to write a hymn specially for the service, little suspecting that it would be sung at countless other confirmations in later years, as well as at other services.

O Jesus, I have promised
To serve Thee to the end;
Be Thou for ever near me,
My master and my friend:
I shall not fear the battle
If Thou art by my side,
Nor wander from the pathway
If Thou wilt be my guide.

O let me feel Thee near me:
The world is ever near;
I see the sights that dazzle,
The tempting sounds I hear;
My foes are ever near me,
Around me and within;
But Jesus, draw Thou nearer,
And shield my soul from sin.

O let me hear Thee speaking
In accents clear and still,
Above the storms of passion,
The murmurs of self-will;
O speak to reassure me,
To hasten, or control;
O speak, and make me listen,
Thou guardian of my soul.

O Jesus, Thou hast promised
To all who follow Thee –
That where Thou art in glory
There shall Thy servant be;
And Jesus, I have promised
To serve Thee to the end;
O give me grace to follow,
My master and my friend.

O let me see Thy footmarks,
And in them plant mine own;
My hope to follow duly
Is in Thy strength alone:
O guide me, call me, draw me,
Uphold me to the end;
And then in heaven receive me,
My Saviour and my friend.

John Ernest Bode (1816–74)

O little town of Bethlehem

This perennially popular Christmas carol was the work of an American preacher, who served in the Episcopal Church in Massachusetts and Philadelphia. He was inspired to write these verses after a pilgrimage to the Holy Land in 1865, specifically after attending a Christmas Eve service at the Church of the Nativity in Bethlehem itself.

O little town of Bethlehem,
How still we see thee lie!
Above thy deep and dreamless sleep
The silent stars go by.
Yet in thy dark streets shineth
The everlasting light;
The hopes and fears of all the years
Are met in thee tonight.

O morning stars, together
Proclaim the holy birth
And praises sing to God the King,
And peace to all the earth.
For Christ is born of Mary;
And, gathered all above,
While mortals sleep, the angels keep
Their watch of wondering love.

How silently, how silently,
The wondrous gift is given!
So God imparts to human hearts
The blessings of His heaven.
No ear may hear His coming;
But in this world of sin,
Where meek souls will receive Him, still
The dear Christ enters in.

Where children pure and happy
Pray to the blessed child,
Where misery cries out to Thee,
Son of the mother mild;
Where charity stands watching
And faith holds wide the door,
The dark night wakes, the glory breaks,
And Christmas comes once more.

O Holy Child of Bethlehem,
Descend to us, we pray;
Cast out our sin, and enter in,
Be born in us today.
We hear the Christmas angels
The great glad tidings tell:
O come to us, abide with us,
Our Lord, Emmanuel.

Phillips Brooks (1835–93)

O love divine

With its focus on love and the imagery of marriage, this hymn is a natural choice for weddings. Considered one of Charles Wesley's finest works, it is much loved for its warm sincerity and depth of expression. Charles' brother John Wesley, in his preface to A Collection of Hymns for the Use of the People called Methodists *(1779) particularly requested editors of hymns to resist attempting to improve on the words of Charles' hymns, as 'none of them is able to mend either the sense or the verse'.*

O love divine, how sweet thou art!
When shall I find my longing heart
All taken up by thee?
I thirst, I faint and die to prove
The greatness of redeeming love,
The love of Christ to me.

Stronger His love than death or hell;
Its riches are unsearchable:
The first-born sons of light
Desire in vain its depths to see;
They cannot reach the mystery,
The length and breadth and height.

God only knows the love of God;
O that it now were shed abroad
In this poor stony heart!
For love I sigh, for love I pine;
This only portion, Lord, be mine,
Be mine this better part.

For ever would I take my seat
With Mary at the master's feet:
Be this my happy choice;
My only care, delight, and bliss,
My joy, my heaven on earth, be this,
To hear the bridegroom's voice.

Charles Wesley (1707–88)

O may I join the choir invisible

George Eliot is usually remembered today for such celebrated novels as The Mill on the Floss *(1860) and* Middlemarch *(1872), but she was also a distinguished poet. 'O may I join the choir invisible' is one of the better known of her poetic works, written in 1867.*

O may I join the choir invisible
Of those immortal dead who live again
In minds made better by their presence:
Live in pulses stirred to generosity,
In deeds of daring rectitude, in scorn
For miserable aims that end with self,
In thoughts sublime that pierce the night like stars,
And with their mild persistence urge man's search
To vaster issues.
So to live is heaven:
To make undying music in the world.
May I reach that purest heaven,
Be to other souls the cup of strength in some great agony,
Enkindle generous ardour, feed pure love,
Beget the smiles that have no cruelty,
Be the sweet presence of a good diffused,
And in diffusion ever more intense.
So shall I join the choir invisible
Whose music is the gladness of the world.

George Eliot (Mary Ann Evans; 1819–80)

O Thou who camest from above

One of the most enduring of the many hymns written by the Methodist hymn writer Charles Wesley, these verses are usually heard today sung to the tune 'Hereford' composed by another Wesley, Charles' grandson Samuel Sebastian Wesley. The use of the word 'inextinguishable' in the second verse, being very difficult to sing, has led to many attempts at rewriting, but the hymn stubbornly remains a favourite.

O Thou who camest from above,
The pure celestial fire to impart,
Kindle a flame of sacred love
On the mean altar of my heart.

There let it for Thy glory burn
With inextinguishable blaze;
And trembling to its source return,
In humble prayer, and fervent praise.

Jesus, confirm my heart's desire
To work, and speak, and think for Thee;
Still let me guard the holy fire,
And still stir up Thy gift in me:

Ready for all Thy perfect will,
My acts of faith and love repeat,
Till death Thy endless mercies seal,
And make my sacrifice complete.

Charles Wesley (1707–88)

The old rugged cross

The American hymn writer George Bennard wrote these verses in Albion, Michigan, in 1913 and they were first sung at Pokagon, also in Michigan, later that year. Bennard was a former member of the Salvation Army who had gone on to join the Methodist Episcopal Church.

On a hill far away stood an old rugged cross,
The emblem of suffering and shame;
And I love that old cross where the dearest and best
For a world of lost sinners was slain.

So I'll cherish the old rugged cross
Till my trophies at last I lay down;
I will cling to the old rugged cross
And exchange it some day for a crown.

O, the old rugged cross, so despised by the world,
Has a wondrous attraction for me;
For the dear Lamb of God left His glory above
To bear it to dark Calvary.

In the old rugged cross, stained with blood so divine,
A wondrous beauty I see;
For 'twas on that old cross Jesus suffered and died
To pardon and sanctify me.

To the old rugged cross I will ever be true,
Its shame and reproach gladly bear;
Then He'll call me some day to my home far away,
When His glory for ever I'll share.

George Bennard (1873–1958)

The Old Vicarage, Grantchester

Rupert Brooke's expression of nostalgic longing in 'The Old Vicarage, Grantchester' has kept it one of nation's favourite poems. Brooke settled in Grantchester, near Cambridge, in 1909 and it subsequently became for him a symbol of all that was cherishable in the English country scene.

Ah God! to see the branches stir
Across the moon at Grantchester!
To smell the thrilling-sweet and rotten
Unforgettable, unforgotten
River-smell, and hear the breeze
Sobbing in the little trees.
Say, do the elm-clumps greatly stand
Still guardians of that holy land?
The chestnuts shade, in reverend dream,
The yet unacademic stream?
Is dawn a secret shy and cold
Anadyomene, silver-gold?
And sunset still a golden sea
From Haslingfield to Madingley?

And after, ere the night is born,
Do hares come out about the corn?
Oh, is the water sweet and cool,
Gentle and brown, above the pool?
And laughs the immortal river still
Under the mill, under the mill?
Say, is there Beauty yet to find?
And Certainty? and Quiet kind?
Deep meadows yet, for to forget
The lies, and truths, and pain? …oh! yet
Stands the Church clock at ten to three?
And is there honey still for tea?

Rupert Brooke (1887–1915)

Once in royal David's city

For many people, Christmas truly begins when the lone choirboy sings the first verse of 'Once in royal David's city' at the outset of the Nine Lessons and Carols service broadcast from King's College, Cambridge every Christmas Eve. Cecil Frances Alexander was a minister's wife who worked with the 'poor, and mean, and lonely' in her husband's parish. Her other hymns included 'All things bright and beautiful' and 'There is a green hill far away'.

Once in royal David's city
Stood a lowly cattle shed,
Where a mother laid her baby,
In a manger for His bed.
Mary was that mother mild,
Jesus Christ her little Child.

He came down to earth from heaven
Who is God and Lord of all,
And His shelter was a stable,
And His cradle was a stall.
With the poor, and mean, and lowly
Lived on earth, our Saviour holy.

And through all His wondrous childhood
He would honour and obey,
Love, and watch the lowly mother
In whose gentle arms He lay.
Christian children all must be
Mild, obedient, good as He.

For He is our childhood's pattern:
Day by day like us He grew;
He was little, weak, and helpless;
Tears and smiles like us He knew;
And He feeleth for our sadness,
And He shareth in our gladness.

And our eyes at last shall see Him,
Through His own redeeming love;
For that child so dear and gentle
Is our Lord in heav'n above;
And He leads His children on
To the place where He is gone.

Not in that poor lowly stable,
With the oxen standing round,
We shall see Him, but in heaven,
Set at God's right hand on high,
When, like stars, His children crowned,
All in white shall wait around.

Cecil Frances Alexander (1818–95)

Once more unto the breach, dear friends

This celebrated speech comes from William Shakespeare's Henry V, *Act III, scene i, where it appears as young King Hal's exhortation to the English troops at the siege of Harfleur. It has since been quoted in part or as a whole, admittedly sometimes ironically, in persuading exhausted soldiers, workers or others to renew their efforts. Laurence Olivier's impassioned delivery of the passage in his 1944 film version of the play remains one of British cinema's most treasured moments.*

Once more unto the breach, dear friends, once more;
Or close the wall up with our English dead!
In peace there's nothing so becomes a man
As modest stillness and humility:
But when the blast of war blows in our ears,
Then imitate the action of the tiger;
Stiffen the sinews, summon up the blood,
Disguise fair nature with hard-favour'd rage;
Then lend the eye a terrible aspect;
Let it pry through the portage of the head
Like the brass cannon; let the brow o'erwhelm it
As fearfully as doth a galled rock
O'erhang and jutty his confounded base,
Swill'd with the wild and wasteful ocean.
Now set the teeth and stretch the nostril wide,
Hold hard the breath, and bend up every spirit
To his full height! On, on, you noblest English!
Whose blood is fet from fathers of war-proof;
Fathers that, like so many Alexanders,
Have in these parts from morn till even fought,
And sheath'd their swords for lack of argument.
Dishonour not your mothers; now attest
That those whom you call'd fathers did beget you.
Be copy now to men of grosser blood,
And teach them how to war. And you, good yeomen,
Whose limbs were made in England, show us here
The mettle of your pasture; let us swear
That you are worth your breeding; which I doubt not;
For there is none of you so mean and base
That hath not noble luster in your eyes.

I see you stand like greyhounds in the slips,
Straining upon the start. The game's afoot:
Follow your spirit; and upon this charge
Cry 'God for Harry! England and Saint George!'

William Shakespeare (1564–1616)

Onward, Christian soldiers

Sabine Baring-Gould was a schoolteacher and curate of Horbury Bridge in Yorkshire and wrote his famous hymn to be sung by Sunday school children on their Whit Monday walk in 1864. It became a great favourite set to a rousing tune by Arthur Sullivan (who is reputed to have been paid just two guineas for his efforts). Once one of the most frequently heard of all hymns, it is now rarely heard on account of its militaristic overtones. Sabine Baring-Gould himself said of his most famous creation: 'It was written in great haste, and I am afraid that some of the rhymes are faulty.'

Onward, Christian soldiers,
Marching as to war,
With the cross of Jesus
Going on before.
Christ the royal Master
Leads against the foe;
Forward into battle,
See, His banner go!

Onward, Christian soldiers,
Marching as to war,
With the cross of Jesus
Going on before.

At the sign of triumph
Satan's legions flee;
On then, Christian soldiers,
On to victory.
Hell's foundations quiver
At the shout of praise;
Brothers, lift your voices,
Loud your anthems raise.

Like a mighty army
Moves the Church of God;
Brothers, we are treading
Where the saints have trod;
We are not divided,
All one body we,
One in hope and doctrine,
One in charity.

Crowns and thrones may perish,
Kingdoms rise and wane,
But the Church of Jesus
Constant will remain;
Gates of hell can never
'Gainst that Church prevail;
We have Christ's own promise,
And that cannot fail.

Onward, then, ye people,
Join our happy throng,
Blend with ours your voices
In the triumph song;
Glory, laud and honour
Unto Christ the King;
This through countless ages
Men and angels sing.

Sabine Baring-Gould (1834–1924)

Our revels now are ended

Prospero's speech from Act IV, scene i of William Shakespeare's last play, The Tempest *(c.1611), ranks among the best-known passages in any of his works. This eloquent meditation upon man's mortality is sometimes quoted at funerals.*

Our revels now are ended. These our actors,
As I foretold you, were all spirits, and
Are melted into air, into thin air;
And, like the baseless fabric of this vision,
The cloud-capped towers, the gorgeous palaces,
The solemn temples, the great globe itself,
Yea, all which it inherit, shall dissolve,
And, like this insubstantial pageant faded,
Leave not a rack behind. We are such stuff
As dreams are made on; and our little life
Is rounded with a sleep.

William Shakespeare (1564–1616)

The parable of the Sower

The parable of the Sower, from Matthew 13:1–9, ranks among the most familiar passages in the Bible. The simple metaphor of the sowing of seeds for the growth of religious faith is easily understood, but the full message concerning the crop resulting from different types of soil was explained for Christ's followers in Matthew 13:18–23.

That same day Jesus went out of the house and sat beside the lake. Such great crowds gathered around him that he got into a boat and sat there, while the whole crowd stood on the beach. And he told them many things in parables, saying: 'Listen! A sower went out to sow. And as he sowed, some seeds fell on the path, and the birds came and ate them up. Other seeds fell on rocky ground, where they did not have much soil, and they sprang up quickly, since they had no depth of soil. But when the sun rose, they were scorched; and since they had no root, they withered away. Other seeds fell among thorns, and the thorns grew up and choked them. Other seeds fell on good soil and brought forth grain, some a hundredfold, some sixty, some thirty. Let anyone with ears listen!'

'Hear then the parable of the sower. When anyone hears the word of the kingdom and does not understand it, the evil one comes and snatches away what is sown in the heart; this is what was sown on the path. As for what was sown on rocky ground, this is the one who hears the word and immediately receives it with joy; yet such a person has no root, but endures only for a while, and when trouble or persecution arises on account of the word, that person immediately falls away. As for what was sown among thorns, this is the one who hears the word, but the cares of the world and the lure of wealth choke the word, and it yields nothing. But as for what was sown on good soil, this is the one who hears the word and understands it, who indeed bears fruit and yields, in one case a hundredfold, in another sixty, and in another thirty.'

Pippa passes

Robert Browning's 'Pippa Passes' ranks among his most popular verse. A straightforward expression of satisfaction and optimism, it may be cited in a wide variety of contexts, though some readers have been known to accuse the poet of complacency and sentimentality.

The year's at the spring,
And day's at the morn;
Morning's at seven;
The hillside's dew-pearled;
The lark's on the wing;
The snail's on the thorn;
God's in His Heaven –
All's right with the world.

Robert Browning (1812–89)

Praise, my soul, the King of heaven

This popular hymn was the work of Henry Francis Lyte, the Devon vicar who also provided the words for such classics as 'Abide with me' and 'God of mercy, God of grace'. The inspiration for his lines, which first appeared in his Spirit of the Psalms (1834) was Psalm 103. The tune was the work of Sir John Goss, organist at St Paul's Cathedral and composer to the Chapel Royal. This hymn was included in the marriage service of Elizabeth II in 1947.

Praise, my soul, the King of heaven,
To His feet thy tribute bring.
Ransomed, healed, restored, forgiven,
Who like me His praise should sing?
Praise Him! Praise Him!
Praise Him! Praise Him!
Praise the everlasting King!

Praise Him for His grace and favour
To our fathers in distress;
Praise Him still the same for ever,
Slow to chide, and swift to bless.
Praise Him! Praise Him!
Praise Him! Praise Him!
Glorious in His faithfulness.

Fatherlike He tends and spares us;
Well our feeble frame He knows;
In His hands He gently bears us,
Rescues us from all our foes.
Praise Him! Praise Him!
Praise Him! Praise Him!
Widely as His mercy flows.

Angels, help us to adore Him;
Ye behold Him face to face;
Sun and moon bow down before Him,
Dwellers all in time and space.
Praise Him! Praise Him!
Praise Him! Praise Him!
Praise with us the God of grace.

Henry Francis Lyte (1793–1847)

Praise to the Lord, the Almighty

The German teacher Joachim Neander wrote some 60 hymns before his premature death from tuberculosis at the age of 30. The words, derived from Psalm 103, reflect his allegiance to the Pietist movement led by his contemporary Philipp Jakob Spener, equivalent to Methodism in the English church. Originally entitled 'Lobe den Herren', the familiar English translation was the work of Catherine Winkworth (1827–78).

Praise to the Lord, the Almighty, the King of creation!
O my soul, praise Him, for He is thy health and salvation:
Come ye who hear,
Brothers and sisters, draw near,
Praise Him in glad adoration!

Praise to the Lord, who o'er all things so wondrously
reigneth,
Shelters thee under His wings, yea, so gently sustaineth:
Hast thou not seen
All that is needful hath been
Granted in what He ordaineth?

Praise to the Lord, who doth prosper thy work and defend
thee!
Surely His goodness and mercy here daily attend thee:
Ponder anew
All the Almighty can do,
He who with love doth befriend thee.

Praise to the Lord, who, when tempests their warfare are
waging,
Who, when the elements madly around thee are raging,
Biddeth them cease,
Turneth their fury to peace,
Whirlwinds and waters assuaging.

Praise to the Lord, who when darkness of sin is abounding,
Who, when the godless do triumph, all virtue confounding,
Sheddeth His light,
Chaseth the horrors of night,
Saints with His mercy surrounding.

Praise to the Lord! O let all that is in me adore Him!
All that hath life and breath come now with praises before
Him!
Let the amen
Sound from His people again:
Gladly for aye we adore Him!

Joachim Neander (1650–80)

Prayer for generosity

This prayer by St Ignatius Loyola is familiar to millions, who have found inspiration in his call for selfless service in the name of the Lord.

Teach us, good Lord, to serve Thee as Thou deservest;
To give and not to count the cost;
To fight and not to heed the wounds;
To toil, and not to seek for rest;
To labour, and to ask for no reward,
Save that of knowing that we do Thy will;
Through Jesus Christ our Lord.

St Ignatius Loyola (1491–1556)

The Prodigal Son

The story of The Prodigal Son, related at Luke 15:11–24, is one of the best-known episodes in the Bible. A moving description of the welcome a loving father gives his long-absent erring son, it is often cited as an illustration of complete forgiveness.

Then Jesus said, "There was a man who had two sons. The younger of them said to his father, 'Father, give me the share of the property that will belong to me.' So he divided his property between them. A few days later the younger son gathered all he had and traveled to a distant country, and there he squandered his property in dissolute living. When he had spent everything, a severe famine took place throughout that country, and he began to be in need. So he went and hired himself out to one of the citizens of that country, who sent him to his fields to feed the pigs. He would gladly have filled himself with the pods that the pigs were eating; and no one gave him anything. But when he came to himself he said, 'How many of my father's hired hands have bread enough and to spare, but here I am dying of hunger! I will get up and go to my father, and I will say to him, "Father, I have sinned against heaven and before you; I am no longer worthy to be called your son; treat me like one of your hired hands." ' So he set off and went to his father. But while he was still far off, his father saw him and was filled with compassion; he ran and put his arms around him and kissed him. Then the son said to him, 'Father, I have sinned against heaven and before you; I am no longer worthy to be called your son.' But the father said to his slaves, 'Quickly, bring out a robe—the best one—and put it on him; put a ring on his finger and sandals on his feet. And get the fatted calf and kill it, and let us eat and celebrate; for this son of mine was dead and is alive again; he was lost and is found!' And they began to celebrate.

The quality of mercy is not strained

This speech, from The Merchant of Venice *(1600), Act IV, scene i, is among the most celebrated passages in any of William Shakespeare's plays. It is often quoted as a reminder that there should be no limit to forgiveness.*

The quality of mercy is not strained;
It droppeth as the gentle rain from heaven
Upon the place beneath: it is twice blessed;
It blesseth him that gives and him that takes:
'Tis mightiest in the mightiest: it becomes
The throned monarch better than his crown;
His sceptre shows the force of temporal power,
The attribute to awe and majesty,
Wherein doth sit the dread and fear of kings;
But mercy is above this sceptred sway;
It is enthroned in the hearts of kings,
It is an attribute to God Himself,
And earthly power doth then show likest God's
When mercy seasons justice.

William Shakespeare (1564–1616)

The race is not to the swift

This passage, from Ecclesiastes 9:1–12, is sometimes cited as support for the argument that life should be lived to the full. This life-affirming message has its own warning, however: all human achievements in life will be forgotten and only God can control the destiny of individuals.

All this I laid to heart, examining it all, how the righteous and the wise and their deeds are in the hand of God; whether it is love or hate one does not know. Everything that confronts them is vanity, since the same fate comes to all, to the righteous and the wicked, to the good and the evil, to the clean and the unclean, to those who sacrifice and those who do not sacrifice. As are the good, so are the sinners; those who swear are like those who shun an oath. This is an evil in all that happens under the sun, that the same fate comes to everyone. Moreover, the hearts of all are full of evil; madness is in their hearts while they live, and after that they go to the dead. But whoever is joined with all the living has hope, for a living dog is better than a dead lion. The living know that they will die, but the dead know nothing; they have no more reward, and even the memory of them is lost. Their love and their hate and their envy have already perished; never again will they have any share in all that happens under the sun.

Go, eat your bread with enjoyment, and drink your wine with a merry heart; for God has long ago approved what you do. Let your garments always be white; do not let oil be lacking on your head. Enjoy life with the wife whom you love, all the days of your vain life that are given you under the sun, because that is your portion in life and in your toil at which you toil under the sun. Whatever your hand finds to do, do with your might; for there is no work or thought or knowledge or wisdom in Sheol, to which you are going.

Again I saw that under the sun the race is not to the swift, nor the battle to the strong, nor bread to the wise, nor riches to the intelligent, nor favour to the skilful; but time and chance happen to them all. For no one can anticipate the time of disaster. Like fish taken in a cruel net, and like birds caught in a snare, so mortals are snared at a time of calamity, when it suddenly falls upon them.

A red, red rose

This poem by the Scottish poet Robert Burns is perhaps his best-known work. Written after his marriage to Jean Armour in 1788, it remains one of the most popular love poems in the English language.

O my love's like a red, red rose
That's newly sprung in June:
O my love's like the melodie
That's sweetly played in tune.

So fair art thou, my bonnie lass,
So deep in love am I;
And I will love thee still, my dear,
Till a' the seas gang dry.

Till a' the seas gang dry, my dear,
And the rocks melt wi' the sun;
I will love thee still, my dear,
While the sands o' life shall run.

And fare thee weel, my only love!
And fare thee weel a while!
And I will come again, my love,
Though it were ten thousand mile.

Robert Burns (1759–96)

Rejoice, the Lord is King

Charles Wesley took as his inspiration for this hymn Paul's letter to the Philippians, in which Paul urged his followers to keep up their spirits even though he was himself imprisoned in Rome. The hymn was originally intended for singing at Easter but is now more often heard around Ascension.

Rejoice, the Lord is King;
Your Lord and King adore;
Mortals, give thanks and sing,
And triumph evermore:

Lift up your heart, lift up your voice:
Rejoice, again I say, rejoice!

Jesus the Saviour reigns,
The God of truth and love;
When He had purged our stains
He took His seat above:

His kingdom cannot fail;
He rules o'er earth and heaven;
The keys of death and hell
Are to our Jesus given:

He sits at God's right hand
Till all His foes submit,
And bow to His command,
And fall beneath His feet:

Rejoice in glorious hope;
Jesus the judge shall come,
And take His servants up
To their eternal home:

We soon shall hear the archangel's voice,
The trump of God shall sound, rejoice!

Charles Wesley (1707–88)

Remember me when I am gone away

This poem by English poet Christina Rossetti is frequently read at funerals as encouragement to the bereaved not to be too sad. Rossetti herself suffered from ill-health throughout her life but actually lived to the age of 64.

Remember me when I am gone away,
Gone far away into the silent land;
When you can no more hold me by the hand,
Nor I half turn to go, yet turning stay.
Remember me when no more day by day
You tell me of our future that you planned:
Only remember me; you understand
It will be late to counsel then or pray.
Yet if you should forget me for a while
And afterwards remember, do not grieve:
For if the darkness and corruption leave
A vestige of the thoughts that once I had,
Better by far you should forget and smile
Than that you should remember and be sad.

Christina Rossetti (1830–94)

Remembrance of things past

This sonnet (Sonnet 30) by William Shakespeare laments times past and friends lost and is consequently occasionally recited at funerals. It also furnished the title for the English translation of Marcel Proust's great novel A la recherche du temps perdu *(1913–27).*

When to the sessions of sweet silent thought
I summon up remembrance of things past,
I sigh the lack of many a thing I sought,
And with old woes new wail my dear time's waste;
Then can I drown an eye, unused to flow,
For precious friends hid in death's dateless night,
And weep afresh love's long-since-cancelled woe,
And moan the expense of many a vanished sight.
Then can I grieve at grievances foregone,
And heavily from woe to woe tell o'er
The sad account of fore-bemoaned moan,
Which I new pay as if not paid before:
    But if the while I think on thee, dear friend,
    All losses are restored, and sorrows end.

William Shakespeare (1564–1616)

Requiem

Robert Louis Stevenson's 'Requiem' is sometimes recited at funerals. Stevenson himself died on the Pacific island of Samoa and, as if in response to his request in these lines, was buried on a hilltop there.

Under the wide and starry sky
Dig the grave and let me lie.
Glad did I live, and gladly die,
And I laid me down with a will.

This be the verse you grave for me:
Here he lies where he longed to be;
Home is the sailor, home from sea,
And the hunter home from the hill.

Robert Louis Stevenson (1850–94)

Resurrection hope

In this passage, 1 Thessalonians 4:13–18, the apostle Paul writes to comfort those whose friends or relatives have died. While grief at their loss is perfectly natural, Paul encourages his readers to look forward to the time when all the followers of Christ, both living and dead, will be with their Lord.

But we do not want you to be uninformed, brothers and sisters, about those who have died, so that you may not grieve as others do who have no hope. For since we believe that Jesus died and rose again, even so, through Jesus, God will bring with him those who have died. For this we declare to you by the word of the Lord, that we who are alive, who are left until the coming of the Lord, will by no means precede those who have died. For the Lord himself, with a cry of command, with the archangel's call and with the sound of God's trumpet, will descend from heaven, and the dead in Christ will rise first. Then we who are alive, who are left, will be caught up in the clouds together with them to meet the Lord in the air; and so we will be with the Lord for ever. Therefore encourage one another with these words.

The road to Emmaus

The story of Christ's appearance at Emmaus, as related at Luke 24:13–37, is a popular Bible reading at Easter, giving proof of Christ's triumph over death.

Now on that same day two of them were going to a village called Emmaus, about seven miles from Jerusalem, and talking with each other about all these things that had happened. While they were talking and discussing, Jesus himself came near and went with them, but their eyes were kept from recognizing him. And he said to them, 'What are you discussing with each other while you walk along?' They stood still, looking sad. Then one of them, whose name was Cleopas, answered him, 'Are you the only stranger in Jerusalem who does not know the things that have taken place there in these days?' He asked them, 'What things?' They replied, 'The things about Jesus of Nazareth, who was a prophet mighty in deed and word before God and all the people, and how our chief priests and leaders handed him over to be condemned to death and crucified him. But we had hoped that he was the one to redeem Israel. Yes, and besides all this, it is now the third day since these things took place. Moreover, some women of our group astounded us. They were at the tomb early this morning, and when they did not find his body there, they came back and told us that they had indeed seen a vision of angels who said that he was alive. Some of those who were with us went to the tomb and found it just as the women had said; but they did not see him.' Then he said to them, 'Oh, how foolish you are, and how slow of heart to believe all that the prophets have declared! Was it not necessary that the Messiah should suffer these things and then enter into his glory?' Then beginning with Moses and all the prophets, he interpreted to them the things about himself in all the scriptures.

As they came near the village to which they were going, he walked ahead as if he were going on. But they urged him strongly, saying, 'Stay with us, because it is almost evening and the day is now nearly over.' So he went in to stay with them. When he was at the table with them, he took bread, blessed and broke it, and gave it to them. Then their eyes were opened, and they recognized him; and he vanished from their sight. They said to each other, 'Were not our hearts burning within us while he was talking to us on the road, while he was opening the scriptures to us?' That same hour they got up and returned to Jerusalem; and they found the eleven and their companions gathered together. They were saying, 'The LORD has risen indeed, and he has appeared to Simon!' Then they told what had happened on the road, and how he had been made known to them in the breaking of the bread.

While they were talking about this, Jesus himself stood among them and said to them, 'Peace be with you.' They were startled and terrified, and thought that they were seeing a ghost.

Rock of ages

Augustus Montague Toplady was a Church of England clergyman who engaged in fiery dispute with the Wesleys and seemed to be obsessed with the topic of sin. He first published this hymn at the end of a magazine article in which he estimated the number of sins committed by an average person to amount to 2,522,880,000. The original reference appears to be to Exodus 33:22, which describes how Moses is hidden in a cleft of rock as God passes by in all his glory.

Rock of ages, cleft for me,
Let me hide myself in Thee;
Let the water and the blood,
From Thy riven side which flowed,
Be of sin the double cure,
Cleanse me from its guilt and power.

Not the labours of my hands
Can fulfil Thy law's demands;
Could my zeal no respite know,
Could my tears for ever flow,
All for sin could not atone;
Thou must save, and Thou alone.

Nothing in my hand I bring;
Simply to Thy cross I cling;
Naked, come to Thee for dress;
Helpless, look to Thee for grace;
Foul, I to the fountain fly;
Wash me, Saviour, or I die.

While I draw this fleeting breath,
When mine eyes shall close in death,
When I soar through tracts unknown,
See Thee on Thy judgement throne;
Rock of ages, cleft for me,
Let me hide myself in Thee.

Augustus Montague Toplady (1740–78)

Rule Britannia

The source of this stirring patriotic song was Act II of a masque by Scottish playwright James Thomson, entitled Alfred *(1740). A shameless piece of patriotic tub-thumping, Thomson's song, set to the music of Thomas Arne, has retained its popularity long after the masque from which it came fell from the repertoire and it is now considered an unofficial second national anthem.*

When Britain first, at heaven's command,
Arose from out the azure main,
This was the charter of the land,
And guardian angels sung this strain:

'Rule, Britannia, rule the waves;
Britons never will be slaves.'

The nations, not so blest as thee,
Must, in their turns, to tyrants fall:
While thou shalt flourish great and free,
The dread and envy of them all.

Still more majestic shalt thou rise,
More dreadful, from each foreign stroke:
As the loud blast that tears the skies,
Serves but to root thy native oak.

Thee haughty tyrants ne'er shall tame:
All their attempts to bend thee down,
Will but arouse thy generous flame;
But work their woe, and thy renown.

To thee belongs the rural reign;
Thy cities shall with commerce shine:
All thine shall be the subject main,
And every shore it circles thine.

The Muses, still with freedom found,
Shall to thy happy coast repair:
Blest isle! with matchless beauty crowned,
And manly hearts to guard the fair.

James Thomson (1700–48)

Say not the struggle naught availeth

This poem by the Victorian poet Arthur Hugh Clough is sometimes cited to encourage the disheartened and bolster flagging resolve. Its message is that no effort is in vain and, even though things may look pessimistic at present, victory may yet be close at hand.

Say not the struggle naught availeth,
The labour and the wounds are vain;
The enemy faints not, nor faileth,
And as things have been they remain.

If hopes were dupes, fears may be liars;
It may be, in yon smoke concealed,
Your comrades chase e'en now the fliers,
And, but for you, possess the field.

For while the tired waves, vainly breaking,
Seem here no painful inch to gain,
Far back, through creeks and inlets making,
Comes silent, flooding in, the main.

And not by eastern windows only,
When daylight comes, comes in the light;
In front the sun climbs slow, how slowly!
But westward, look, the land is bright!

Arthur Hugh Clough (1819–61)

Search me, O God, and know my heart

This passage from Psalm 139:1-23 emphasizes the unknowable, all-seeing nature of God and the impossibility of understanding those things that only God knows. The psalmist acknowledges what an awesome thing it is to ask God to examine one's very soul, but at the same time declares that God knows every thought, word and deed and there is no hiding place, no darkness that can conceal anything from God.

O LORD, you have searched me and known me.
You know when I sit down and when I rise up;
  you discern my thoughts from far away.
You search out my path and my lying down,
  and are acquainted with all my ways.
Even before a word is on my tongue,
  O LORD, you know it completely.
You hem me in, behind and before,
  and lay your hand upon me.
Such knowledge is too wonderful for me;
  it is so high that I cannot attain it.
Where can I go from your spirit?
  Or where can I flee from your presence?
If I ascend to heaven, you are there;
  if I make my bed in Sheol, you are there.
If I take the wings of the morning
  and settle at the farthest limits of the sea,
even there your hand shall lead me,
  and your right hand shall hold me fast.
If I say, 'Surely the darkness shall cover me,
  and the light around me become night',
even the darkness is not dark to you;
  the night is as bright as the day, for darkness is as light to you.
For it was you who formed my inward parts;
  you knit me together in my mother's womb.
I praise you, for I am fearfully and wonderfully made.
  Wonderful are your works; that I know very well.
My frame was not hidden from you,
  when I was being made in secret,
  intricately woven in the depths of the earth.

Your eyes beheld my unformed substance.
In your book were written all the days that were formed for me,
when none of them as yet existed.
How weighty to me are your thoughts, O God!
How vast is the sum of them!
I try to count them – they are more than the sand;
I come to the end – I am still with you.
O that you would kill the wicked, O God,
and that the bloodthirsty would depart from me –
those who speak of you maliciously,
and lift themselves up against you for evil!
Do I not hate those who hate you, O LORD?
And do I not loathe those who rise up against you?
I hate them with perfect hatred;
I count them my enemies.
Search me, O God, and know my heart;
test me and know my thoughts.

Shall I compare thee to a summer's day

William Shakespeare's 'Sonnet 18' can justifiably claim to be the most revered piece of love poetry in the English language. Even those who never read poetry are likely to know at least the first line of this verse.

Shall I compare thee to a summer's day?
Thou art more lovely and more temperate.
Rough winds do shake the darling buds of May,
And summer's lease hath all too short a date.
Sometime too hot the eye of heaven shines,
And often is his gold complexion dimmed;
And every fair from fair sometime declines,
By chance, or nature's changing course, untrimmed;
But thy eternal summer shall not fade,
Nor lose possession of that fair thou ow'st,
Nor shall Death brag thou wand'rest in his shade,
When in eternal lines to time thou grow'st.
So long as men can breathe or eyes can see,
So long lives this, and this gives life to thee.

William Shakespeare (1564–1616)

The shepherd boy sings in the valley of humiliation

This poem by the English preacher and writer John Bunyan expresses the assurance and contentment that faith can bring. Bunyan himself wrote from experience, having to fall back on his religious convictions at times of distress at various times in his life, notably after his first wife died around 1656 (leaving him with four children) and when he was imprisoned in Bedford gaol for some 12 years after being arrested for preaching without a licence.

He that is down needs fear no fall,
He that is low, no pride;
He that is humble ever shall
Have God to be his guide.

I am content with what I have,
Little be it or much;
And, Lord, contentment still I crave,
Because Thou savest such.

Fullness to such a burden is
That go on pilgrimage;
Here little, and hereafter bliss,
Is best from age to age.

John Bunyan (1628–88)

Silent night

This most famous of carols came into existence as a consequence of the church organ in the Austrian village of Unterweisburg breaking down at Christmas 1818. To solve the problem, the village's young curate Joseph Mohr rapidly composed some seasonal verses and asked Franz Grüber, his organist, to write some simple guitar music to accompany them. The resulting carol was first performed at St Nicholas Church in Unterweisburg on Christmas Eve and became an immediate favourite.

Their creation was translated into English by John Freeman Young (1820–85) and legend has it that at Christmas 1914 it was this carol that opposing British and German forces in the trenches of World War I famously joined in singing in their different languages in a spontaneous seasonal lull in combat.

Silent night, holy night,
All is calm, all is bright
Round yon virgin mother and Child.
Holy Infant so tender and mild,
Sleep in heavenly peace,
Sleep in heavenly peace.

Silent night, holy night,
Shepherds quake at the sight.
Glories stream from heaven afar,
Heavenly hosts sing alleluia;
Christ the Saviour is born!
Christ the Saviour is born!

Silent night, holy night,
Son of God, love's pure light
Radiant beams from Thy holy face,
With the dawn of redeeming grace,
Jesus, Lord, at Thy birth,
Jesus, Lord, at Thy birth.

Joseph Mohr (1792–1848)

The Soldier

This celebrated poem published early in 1915 is synonymous with the destruction of a generation of young Englishmen in World War I, whose countless victims were to include Rupert Brooke himself. The patriotic, even jingoistic sentiments of the poem reflect the determined optimism with which the nation entered the war, its author – a commissioned officer in the British army – dying before the full horror of the conflict was generally appreciated. He was laid to rest in his own 'corner of a foreign field' on the island of Skyros after he died of blood-poisoning on his way to the Dardanelles.

If I should die, think only this of me:
That there's some corner of a foreign field
That is for ever England. There shall be
In that rich earth a richer dust concealed;
A dust whom England bore, shaped, made aware,
Gave, once, her flowers to love, her ways to roam,
A body of England's, breathing English air,
Washed by the rivers, blest by suns of home.

And think, this heart, all evil shed away,
A pulse in the eternal mind, no less
Gives somewhere back the thoughts by England given;
Her sights and sounds; dreams happy as her day;
And laughter, learnt of friends; and gentleness,
In hearts at peace, under an English heaven.

Rupert Brooke (1887–1915)

Soldiers of Christ, arise

Charles Wesley wrote this evangelizing hymn in 1749, originally giving it the title 'The Whole armour of God'. It was based upon Paul's letter to the Ephesians, which included the lines: 'Put on the whole armour of God, that ye may be able to stand against the wiles of the devil.'

Soldiers of Christ, arise,
And put your armour on,
Strong in the strength which God supplies
Through His eternal Son;
Strong in the Lord of hosts,
And in His mighty power;
Who in the strength of Jesus trusts
Is more than conqueror.

Stand, then, in His great might,
With all His strength endued;
And take, to arm you for the fight,
The panoply of God.
Leave no unguarded place,
No weakness of the soul:
Take every virtue, every grace,
And fortify the whole.

From strength to strength go on;
Wrestle, and fight, and pray;
Tread all the powers of darkness down,
And win the well-fought day, –
That, having all things done,
And all your conflicts passed,
Ye may o'ercome through Christ alone,
And stand entire at last.

Charles Wesley (1707–88)

The Song of Solomon

These lines from the Song of Solomon 4:1–7 have long been remarked upon for their strong poetic character. They remain one of the most fluent and evocative passages celebrating romantic love anywhere in biblical literature.

How beautiful you are, my love,
    how very beautiful!
    Your eyes are doves behind your veil.
    Your hair is like a flock of goats,
    moving down the slopes of Gilead.
Your teeth are like a flock of shorn ewes
    that have come up from the washing,
    all of which bear twins,
    and not one among them is bereaved.
Your lips are like a crimson thread,
    and your mouth is lovely.
Your cheeks are like halves of a pomegranate
    behind your veil.
Your neck is like the tower of David,
    built in courses;
    on it hang a thousand bucklers,
    all of them shields of warriors.
Your two breasts are like two fawns,
    twins of a gazelle,
    that feed among the lilies.
Until the day breathes and the shadows flee,
    I will hasten to the mountain of myrrh
    and the hill of frankincense.
You are altogether beautiful, my love;
    there is no flaw in you.

Stand up! stand up for Jesus

This enduringly popular hymn, written by a US clergyman, had its origins in a tragic farm accident involving the Reverend Dudley Atkins Tyng, rector of the Church of the Epiphany in Philadelphia. Renowned for his public denunciations of slavery, Tyng had been forced to relinquish his parish but continued to stage mass meetings against slavery. In the midst of this campaign, while visiting a local farm, Tyng's long sleeve became entangled in some agricultural machinery and his arm was wrenched off. When George Duffield visited Tyng on his deathbed the dying man asked him to pass on a final message to his flock: 'Tell them to stand up for Jesus!' Inspired by this sentiment, Duffield composed the following lines for his friend's funeral.

Stand up! – stand up for Jesus,
Ye soldiers of the cross!
Lift high His royal banner,
It must not suffer loss.
From victory unto victory
His army He shall lead,
Till every foe is vanquished
And Christ is Lord indeed.

Stand up! – stand up for Jesus!
The trumpet call obey,
Forth to the mighty conflict
In this His glorious day.
Ye that are men, now serve Him
Against unnumbered foes;
Let courage rise with danger,
And strength with strength oppose.

Stand up! – stand up for Jesus!
Stand in His strength alone;
The arm of flesh will fail you,
Ye dare not trust your own.
Put on the gospel armour,
Each piece put on with prayer;
Where duty calls or danger,
Be never wanting there!

Stand up! – stand up for Jesus!
The strife will not be long;
This day the noise of battle,
The next the victor's song.
To him that overcometh
A crown of life shall be;
He with the King of glory
Shall reign eternally.

George Duffield (1818–88)

Stone walls do not a prison make

This poem of defiance against incarceration, entitled 'To Althea, from prison', was inspired by personal experience. It was written by the English courtier and poet Richard Lovelace in London's Gatehouse prison, into which he had been thrown in 1642 by his Parliamentarian enemies. Unfortunately for the author, 'Althea' (his name for his intended bride, Lucy Sacheverell) was later incorrectly told that Lovelace had died and so married someone else.

When Love with unconfined wings
Hovers within my gates,
And my divine Althea brings
To whisper at the grates;
When I lie tangled in her hair
And fetter'd to her eye,
The birds that wanton in the air
Know no such liberty.

When flowing cups run swiftly round
With no allaying Thames,
Our careless heads with roses crown'd,
Our hearts with loyal flames;
When thirsty grief in wine we steep,
When healths and draughts go free –
Fishes that tipple in the deep
Know no such liberty.

When, linnet-like confined, I
With shriller throat shall sing
The sweetness, mercy, majesty
And glories of my King;
When I shall voice aloud how good
He is, how great should be,
Enlargèd winds, that curl the flood,
Know no such liberty.

Stone walls do not a prison make,
Nor iron bars a cage;
Minds innocent and quiet take
That for an hermitage:
If I have freedom in my love
And in my soul am free,
Angels alone, that soar above,
Enjoy such liberty.

Richard Lovelace (1618–57)

Sweet spirit, comfort me

This plea by English poet Robert Herrick for divine comfort reflected his own turbulent life story. The misfortunes he had to endure included the apparent suicide of his father while Robert was still an infant, military defeat in France, isolation from his beloved London as Dean Prior in rural Devon and ejection from his living there by Parliamentarian opponents in 1647.

In the houre of my distresse,
When temptations me oppresse,
And when I my sins confesse,
Sweet spirit, comfort me!

When I lie within my bed,
Sick in heart and sick in head,
And with doubts discomforted,
Sweet spirit, comfort me!

When the house doth sigh and weep,
And the world is drowned in sleep,
Yet mine eyes the watch do keep,
Sweet spirit, comfort me!

Robert Herrick (1591–1674)

Swing low, sweet chariot

This traditional spiritual is familiar to millions and has been sung in countless different ways and contexts, from revivalist church meetings to pop concerts. Its cheerful approach to the coming of death offers consolation to those who fear their own demise.

Swing low, sweet chariot,
Comin' for to carry me home,
Swing low, sweet chariot,
Comin' for to carry me home.

I looked over Jordan, and what did I see
Comin' for to carry me home?
A band of angels comin' after me,
Comin' for to carry me home.

If you get there before I do,
Comin' for to carry me home;
Tell all my friends I'm comin' too
Comin' for to carry me home.

I'm sometimes up and sometimes down
Comin' for to carry me home;
But still my soul feels heavenly bound,
Comin' for to carry me home.

Yet my soul feels heav'nly bound
Comin' for to carry me home
Swing low, sweet chariot
Comin' for to carry me home.

Anonymous

Take my life, and let it be

Frances Ridley Havergal was the spinster daughter of a Worcestershire rector and wrote a number of popular hymns, of which this is one of the best known. She composed these lines in 1874 as a consecration hymn while enjoying a holiday visit to friends at the age of 37 and, finding herself unable to sleep, pondered the influence of God on all the different aspects of her life.

Take my life, and let it be
Consecrated, Lord, to Thee;
Take my moments and my days,
Let them flow in ceaseless praise.

Take my hands, and let them move
At the impulse of Thy love;
Take my feet, and let them be
Swift and beautiful for Thee.

Take my voice, and let me sing
Always, only, for my King;
Take my lips, and let them be
Filled with messages from Thee.

Take my silver and my gold,
Not a mite would I withhold;
Take my intellect, and use
Every power as Thou shalt choose.

Take my will, and make it Thine:
It shall be no longer mine.
Take my heart – it is Thine own;
It shall be Thy royal throne.

Take my love; my Lord, I pour
At Thy feet its treasure-store;
Take myself, and I will be,
Ever, only, all for Thee.

Frances Ridley Havergal (1836–79)

Tell me not, in mournful numbers

This poem by Henry Wadsworth Longfellow urges his readers to seize life and make the most of their opportunities. Longfellow himself was acutely conscious of the temporary nature of existence, losing his first wife at a young age while travelling in Holland in 1835 and his second wife in a tragic domestic accident in 1861.

Tell me not, in mournful numbers,
Life is but an empty dream,
For the soul is dead that slumbers,
And things are not what they seem.

Life is real! Life is earnest!
And the grave is not its goal;
Dust thou art, to dust returnest,
Was not spoken of the soul.

Not enjoyment, and not sorrow,
Is our destined end or way;
But to act that each tomorrow
Finds us farther than today.

Art is long and Time is fleeting,
And our hearts, though stout and brave,
Still, like muffled drums, are beating
Funeral marches to the grave.

In the world's broad field of battle,
In the bivouac of Life,
Be not like dumb driven cattle;
Be a hero in the strife!

Lives of great men all remind us
We can make our lives sublime,
And, departing, leave behind us
Footprints on the sands of Time:

Footprints that perhaps another,
Sailing o'er life's solemn main,
A forlorn and shipwrecked brother,
Seeing, shall take heart again.

Let us, then, be up and doing,
With a heart for any fate:
Still achieving, still pursuing,
Learn to labour and to wait.

Henry Wadsworth Longfellow (1807–82)

Tell me the old, old story

Arabella Catherine Hankey turned to the church after travelling to South Africa to bring home her brother, wounded in the Boer War, and witnessing the work being done by missionaries abroad. The permanent popularity of her lines was established after they were set to music composed during a long stagecoach journey by the US composer W. H. Doane. The addition of a chorus written by Doane did not go down well initially with Hankey, who felt a chorus was unnecessary, but she eventually resigned herself to his changes when she realized how popular his version was.

Tell me the old, old story
Of unseen things above,
Of Jesus and His glory,
Of Jesus and His love:
Tell me the story simply,
As to a little child,
For I am weak and weary,
And helpless and defiled.

Tell me the old, old story,
Tell me the old, old story,
Tell me the old, old story,
Of Jesus and His love.

Tell me the story slowly,
That I may take it in –
That wonderful redemption,
God's remedy for sin.
Tell me the story often,
For I forget so soon;
The early dew of morning
Has passed away at noon.

Tell me the story softly,
With earnest tones and grave:
Remember, I'm the sinner
Whom Jesus came to save.
Tell me that story always,
If you would really be,
In any time of trouble,
A comforter to me.

Tell me the same old story
When you have cause to fear
That this world's empty glory
Is costing me too dear.
Yes, and when that world's glory
Is dawning on my soul,
Tell me the old, old story –
Christ Jesus makes thee whole.

Arabella Catherine Hankey (1834–1911)

Tell out, my soul, the greatness of the Lord

This is a relatively late addition to the canon of established hymns, being written as recently as 1961 by Timothy Dudley-Smith, later Bishop of Thetford. The first line of the hymn comes from the Magnificat in the New English Bible (Luke 1:46). The hymn was described by John Betjeman as 'one of the very few new hymns really to establish themselves in recent years'. It is usually sung to the tune 'Woodlands' by Walter Greatorex (d.1949).

Tell out, my soul, the greatness of the Lord!
Unnumbered blessings, give my spirit voice;
Tender to me the promise of His word;
In God my Saviour shall my heart rejoice.

Tell out, my soul, the greatness of His name!
Make known His might, the deeds His arm has done;
His mercy sure, from age to age the same;
His holy name, the Lord, the Mighty One.

Tell out, my soul, the greatness of His might!
Powers and dominions lay their glory by.
Proud hearts and stubborn wills are put to flight,
The hungry fed, the humble lifted high.

Tell out, my soul, the glories of His word!
Firm is His promise, and His mercy sure.
Tell out, my soul, the greatness of the Lord
To children's children and for evermore!

Timothy Dudley-Smith (b.1926)

There is a green hill far away

The story goes that minister's wife Cecil Frances Alexander took up hymn writing after one of her godchildren admitted having difficulty learning the catechism. It was in an effort to make such chores easier that she went on to compose such well-loved hymns as 'All Things Bright and Beautiful' and 'Once in royal David's city'. It is said that the green hill that inspired this particular classic was a grassy hill on the edge of Londonderry that, in Alexander's mind, came to symbolize Jerusalem's Calvary (which she never actually saw).

There is a green hill far away,
Without a city wall,
Where the dear Lord was crucified,
Who died to save us all.

We may not know, we cannot tell,
What pains He had to bear,
But we believe it was for us
He hung and suffered there.

He died that we might be forgiven,
He died to make us good,
That we might go at last to heaven,
Saved by His precious blood.

There was no other good enough
To pay the price of sin;
He only could unlock the gate
Of heaven, and let us in.

O dearly, dearly has He loved,
And we must love Him too,
And trust in His redeeming blood,
And try His works to do.

Cecil Frances Alexander (1818–95)

There is no death!

J. L. McCreery's poem defying the power of death has proved itself an enduring favourite over the years. The story goes that McCreery himself enjoyed the mysterious gift of knowing in advance whenever there was a death imminent in his own extended family.

There is no death! The stars go down
To rise upon some fairer shore:
And bright in heaven's jewelled crown
They shine for evermore.

There is no death! The dust we tread
Shall change beneath the summer showers
To golden grain or mellowed fruit,
Or rainbow-tinted flowers.

There is no death! The leaves may fall,
And flowers may fade and pass away;
They only wait, through wintry hours,
The coming of the May.

And ever near us, though unseen,
The dear immortal spirits tread;
For all the boundless universe
Is life – there are no dead.

John Luckey McCreery (1835–1906)

There is therefore now no condemnation

These verses, Romans 8:1–4 and 26–27, come from a section of Paul's letter dealing with the work of the Spirit in the life of the Christian. Having received the Spirit into our lives, a new relationship begins and believers are freed to live in the life of the Spirit rather than under the legalism of the old covenant. Verses 26–27 describe how the Spirit is at work in the prayers of the faithful.

There is therefore now no condemnation for those who are in Christ Jesus. For the law of the Spirit of life in Christ Jesus has set you free from the law of sin and death. For God has done what the law, weakened by the flesh, could not do: by sending his own Son in the likeness of sinful flesh, and to deal with sin, he condemned sin in the flesh, so that the just requirement of the law might be fulfilled in us, who walk not according to the flesh but according to the Spirit.

Likewise the Spirit helps us in our weakness; for we do not know how to pray as we ought, but that very Spirit intercedes with sighs too deep for words. And God, who searches the heart, knows what is the mind of the Spirit, because the Spirit intercedes for the saints according to the will of God.

There'll always be an England

'There'll always be an England' ranks high among the anthems of flag-waving English patriots. Its old-fashioned imagery and nostalgia for an ideal imperial past, however, means it has come to be particularly identified with conservative middle-class England and for many people the song carries with it negative connotations of complacency and arrogance.

There'll always be an England,
While there's a country lane.
Wherever there's a cottage small
Beside a field of grain.

There'll always be an England
While there's a busy street.
Wherever there's a turning wheel
A million marching feet.

Red, white and blue
What does it mean to you?
Surely you're proud
Shout it loud
Britons awake!

The Empire too
We can depend on you.
Freedom remains
These are the chains
Nothing can break.

There'll always be an England
And England shall be free
If England means as much to you
As England means to me.

Clarke Ross Parker (1914–74)

They shall not grow old

Laurence Binyon wrote this poem in tribute to the soldiers who died fighting for Britain in World War I. The stanza beginning 'They shall not grow old' is widely familiar from its repetition at Remembrance Day services and on other similar solemn occasions, although the rest of the poem is rarely heard.

With proud thanksgiving, a mother for her children,
England mourns for her dead across the sea.
Flesh of her flesh they were, spirit of her spirit,
Fallen in the cause of the free.

Solemn the drums thrill; Death august and royal
Sings sorrow up into immortal spheres.
There is music in the midst of desolation
And a glory that shines upon our tears.

They went with songs to the battle, they were young,
Straight of limb, true of eye, steady and aglow.
They were staunch to the end against odds uncounted,
They fell with their faces to the foe.

They shall grow not old, as we who are left grow old:
Age shall not weary them, nor the years condemn.
At the going down of the sun and in the morning
We shall remember them.

They mingle not with their laughing comrades again;
They sit no more at familiar tables of home;
They have no lot in our labour of the day-time;
They sleep beyond England's foam.

But where our desires are and our hopes profound,
Felt as a well-spring that is hidden from sight,
To the innermost heart of their own land they are known
As the stars are known to the Night;

As the stars that shall be bright when we are dust,
Moving in marches upon the heavenly plain,
As the stars that are starry in the time of our darkness,
To the end, to the end, they remain.

Laurence Binyon (1869–1943)

Thine be the glory

Edmond Budry, pastor of the Protestant Church at Vevey in Switzerland, published this hymn in 1904 but it was in its English translation by Richard Hoyle (1875–1939) that it became really popular. Sung by Catholics and Protestants with equal enthusiasm, it is set to the march 'See the conquering hero comes' from the Handel oratorio Judas Maccabaeus (1746).

Thine be the glory, risen, conquering Son,
Endless is the victory Thou o'er death hast won;
Angels in bright raiment rolled the stone away,
Kept the folded grave-clothes where Thy body lay.

Thine be the glory, risen, conquering Son,
Endless is the victory Thou o'er death hast won.

Lo, Jesus meets us, risen from the tomb;
Lovingly He greets us, scatters fear and gloom;
Let the Church with gladness hymns of triumph sing,
For her Lord now liveth, death hath lost its sting:

No more we doubt Thee, glorious Prince of Life;
Life is naught without Thee: aid us in our strife;
Make us more than conquerors through Thy deathless love;
Bring us safe through Jordan to Thy home above:

Edmond Budry (1854–1932)

Those who are first will be last

In this biblical passage, from Mark 10:17–31, Christ describes the commitment needed to follow him. Worldly attachments must be set aside, with following Christ becoming the disciple's priority. The instruction that the rich must give away their possessions remains as challenging a demand today as it clearly was at the time it was first made.

As he was setting out on a journey, a man ran up and knelt before him, and asked him, 'Good Teacher, what must I do to inherit eternal life?' Jesus said to him, 'Why do you call me good? No one is good but God alone. You know the commandments: "You shall not murder; You shall not commit adultery; You shall not steal; You shall not bear false witness; You shall not defraud; Honour your father and mother."' He said to him, 'Teacher, I have kept all these since my youth.' Jesus, looking at him, loved him and said, 'You lack one thing; go, sell what you own, and give the money to the poor, and you will have treasure in heaven; then come, follow me.' When he heard this, he was shocked and went away grieving, for he had many possessions.

Then Jesus looked around and said to his disciples, 'How hard it will be for those who have wealth to enter the kingdom of God!' And the disciples were perplexed at these words. But Jesus said to them again, 'Children, how hard it is to enter the kingdom of God! It is easier for a camel to go through the eye of a needle than for someone who is rich to enter the kingdom of God.' They were greatly astounded and said to one another, 'Then who can be saved?' Jesus looked at them and said, 'For mortals it is impossible, but not for God; for God all things are possible.'

Peter began to say to him, 'Look, we have left everything and followed you.' Jesus said, 'Truly I tell you, there is no one who has left house or brothers or sisters or mother or father or children or fields, for my sake and for the sake of the good news, who will not receive a hundredfold now in this age – houses, brothers and sisters, mothers and children, and fields, with persecutions – and in the age to come eternal life. But many who are first will be last, and the last will be first.'

The three wise men

The story of the three wise men, as related at Matthew 2:1–12, is one of the readings traditionally read in churches throughout the Christian world during the Christmas period.

In the time of King Herod, after Jesus was born in Bethlehem of Judea, wise men from the East came to Jerusalem, asking, 'Where is the child who has been born king of the Jews? For we observed his star at its rising, and have come to pay him homage.' When King Herod heard this, he was frightened, and all Jerusalem with him; and calling together all the chief priests and scribes of the people, he inquired of them where the Messiah was to be born. They told him, 'In Bethlehem of Judea; for so it has been written by the prophet:

"And you, Bethlehem, in the land of Judah,
    are by no means least among the rulers of Judah;
    for from you shall come a ruler
    who is to shepherd my people Israel."'

Then Herod secretly called for the wise men and learned from them the exact time when the star had appeared. Then he sent them to Bethlehem, saying, 'Go and search diligently for the child; and when you have found him, bring me word so that I may also go and pay him homage.' When they had heard the king, they set out; and there, ahead of them, went the star that they had seen at its rising, until it stopped over the place where the child was. When they saw that the star had stopped, they were overwhelmed with joy. On entering the house, they saw the child with Mary his mother; and they knelt down and paid him homage. Then, opening their treasure-chests, they offered him gifts of gold, frankincense, and myrrh. And having been warned in a dream not to return to Herod, they left for their own country by another road.

Through all the changing scenes of life

Based on Psalm 34, this hymn was the result of the collaboration of two Irish clergymen, Nicholas Brady and Nahum Tate, upon a 'New Version' of the psalms, published in 1696. Brady was chaplain to William and Mary and subsequently to Queen Anne, while Tate became Poet Laureate, usually remembered today for his rewriting of Shakespeare's tragedies to make them more suitable to 'refined' audiences of his time.

Through all the changing scenes of life,
In trouble and in joy,
The praises of my God shall still
My heart and tongue employ.

Of His deliverance I will boast,
Till all that are distressed
From my example comfort take,
And charm their griefs to rest.

O magnify the Lord with me,
With me exalt His name;
When in distress to Him I called,
He to my rescue came.

The hosts of God encamp around
The dwellings of the just;
Deliverance He affords to all
Who on His succour trust.

O make but trial of His love;
Experience will decide
How blest are they, and only they,
Who in His truth confide.

Fear Him, ye saints, and you will then
Have nothing else to fear;
Make you His service your delight,
Your wants shall be His care.

Nahum Tate (1652–1715) and Nicholas Brady (1659–1726)

Till the sun grows cold

The US poet Bayard Taylor's expression of undying love in this poem has kept it in popular circulation into modern times. Taylor, incidentally, knew well the landscape he describes here, being a well-respected travel-writer whose wanderings took him through the deserts of Asia Minor and Syria and elsewhere.

From the desert I come to thee
On a stallion shod with fire,
And the winds are left behind
In the speed of my desire.
Under thy window I stand,
And the midnight hears my cry:
I love thee, I love but thee,
With a love that shall not die
    Till the sun grows cold,
    And the stars are old,
    And the leaves of the Judgment Book unfold!

Look from thy window and see
My passion and my pain;
I lie on the sands below,
And I faint in thy disdain.
Let the night winds touch thy brow
With the heat of my burning sigh,
And melt thee to hear the vow
Of a love that shall not die
    Till the sun grows cold,
    And the stars are old,
    And the leaves of the Judgment Book unfold!

My steps are nightly driven,
By the fever in my breast,
To hear from thy lattice breathed
The word that shall give me rest.
Open the door of thy heart,
And open thy chamber door,
And my kisses shall teach thy lips
The love that shall fade no more
    Till the sun grows cold,
    And the stars are old,
    And the leaves of the Judgment Book unfold!

Bayard Taylor (1825–78)

To a good man of most dear memory

William Wordsworth's epitaph to the essayist and poet Charles Lamb has long been considered one of the most eloquent and moving of all literary epitaphs. Parts of it have sometimes been quoted in tribute to other notable people.

To a good Man of most dear memory
This Stone is sacred. Here he lies apart
From the great city where he first drew breath,
Was reared and taught; and humbly earned his bread,
To the strict labours of the merchant's desk
By duty chained. Not seldom did those tasks
Tease, and the thought of time so spent depress,
His spirit, but the recompence was high;
Firm Independence, Bounty's rightful sire;
Affections, warm as sunshine, free as air;
And when the precious hours of leisure came,
Knowledge and wisdom, gained from converse sweet
With books, or while he ranged the crowded streets
With a keen eye, and overflowing heart:
So genius triumphed over seeming wrong,
And poured out truth in works by thoughtful love
Inspired – works potent over smiles and tears.
And as round mountain-tops the lightning plays,
Thus innocently sported, breaking forth
As from a cloud of some grave sympathy,
Humour and wild instinctive wit, and all
The vivid flashes of his spoken words.
From the most gentle creature nursed in fields
Had been derived the name he bore – a name
Wherever Christian altars have been raised,
Hallowed to meekness and to innocence;
And if in him meekness at times gave way,
Provoked out of herself by troubles strange,
Many and strange, that hung about his life;
Still, at the centre of his being, lodged
A soul by resignation sanctified:
And if too often, self-reproached, he felt

That innocence belongs not to our kind,
A power that never ceased to abide in him,
Charity, mid the multitude of sins
That she can cover, left not his exposed
To an unforgiving judgment from just Heaven.
O, he was good, if e'er a good Man lived!

William Wordsworth (1770–1850)

To God be the glory

Written around 1872, this rousing evangelical hymn reflects the irrepressible optimism of the blind hymn writer Fanny Crosby. It fell from favour in the first half of the twentieth century but became widely familiar on both sides of the Atlantic once more after it was taken up by US evangelist Billy Graham during his crusades of the 1950s.

To God be the glory, great things He hath done!
So loved He the world that He gave us His Son,
Who yielded His life in atonement for sin,
And opened the life-gate that all may go in.

Praise the Lord! Praise the Lord! Let the earth hear His voice!
Praise the Lord! Praise the Lord! Let the people rejoice!
O come to the Father, through Jesus the Son;
And give Him the glory – great things He hath done!

O perfect redemption, the purchase of blood,
To every believer the promise of God!
The vilest offender who truly believes,
That moment from Jesus a pardon receives.

Great things He hath taught us, great things He hath done,
And great our rejoicing through Jesus the Son;
But purer and higher and greater will be
Our wonder, our rapture, when Jesus we see.

Fanny Crosby (Frances van Alstyne; 1820–1915)

To his coy mistress

This celebrated poem by English poet Andrew Marvell famously makes the point that life is brief and that it is a mistake not to make the most of opportunity while it is there.

Had we but world enough, and time,
This coyness, lady, were no crime.
We would sit down, and think which way
To walk, and pass our long love's day.
Thou by the Indian Ganges' side
Should'st rubies find: I by the tide
Of Humber would complain. I would
Love you ten years before the Flood,
And you should, if you please, refuse
Till the conversion of the Jews.
My vegetable love should grow
Vaster than empires, and more slow.
An hundred years should go to praise
Thine eyes, and on thy forehead gaze:
Two hundred to adore each breast;
But thirty thousand to the rest;
An age at least to every part,
And the last age should show your heart.
For, lady, you deserve this state,
Nor would I love at lower rate.
    But at my back I always hear
Time's winged chariot hurrying near:
And yonder all before us lie
Deserts of vast eternity.
Thy beauty shall no more be found;
Nor, in thy marble vault, shall sound
My echoing song: then worms shall try
That long-preserved virginity,
And your quaint honour turn to dust,
And into ashes all my lust.
The grave's a fine and private place,
But none, I think, do there embrace.
    Now, therefore, while the youthful hue
Sits on thy skin like morning dew,

And while thy willing soul transpires
At every pore with instant fires,
Now let us sport us while we may;
And now, like amorous birds of prey,
Rather at once our Time devour,
Than languish in his slow-chapt power.
Let us roll all our strength and all
Our sweetness up into one ball,
And tear our pleasures with rough strife
Through the iron gates of life.
Thus, though we cannot make our Sun
Stand still, yet we will make him run.

Andrew Marvell (1621–74)

To the virgins, to make much of time

Robert Herrick's message in this poem is very clear: life is short and time that is wasted, especially in youth, can never be reclaimed.

Gather ye rosebuds while ye may,
Old Time is still a-flying:
And this same flower that smiles to-day
To-morrow will be dying.

The glorious lamp of heaven, the sun,
The higher he's a-getting,
The sooner will his race be run,
And nearer he's to setting.

That age is best which is the first,
When youth and blood are warmer;
But being spent, the worse, and worst
Times still succeed the former.

Then be not coy, but use your time,
And while ye may, go marry:
For having lost but once your prime,
You may for ever tarry.

Robert Herrick (1591–1674)

To thine own self be true

This speech comes from William Shakespeare's tragedy Hamlet *(c.1601), Act I, scene iii, in which it is voiced by Polonius.*

Yet here, Laertes! Aboard, aboard for shame!
The wind sits in the shoulder of your sail,
And you are stay'd for.
There ... my blessing with thee!
And these few precepts in thy memory
Look thou character. Give thy thoughts no tongue,
Nor any unproportion'd thought his act.
Be thou familiar, but by no means vulgar.
Those friends thou hast, and their adoption tried,
Grapple them to thy soul with hoops of steel;
But do not dull thy palm with entertainment
Of each new-hatch'd, unfledg'd comrade. Beware
Of entrance to a quarrel but, being in,
Bear't that th' opposed may beware of thee.
Give every man thy ear, but few thy voice;
Take each man's censure, but reserve thy judgment.
Costly thy habit as thy purse can buy,
But not express'd in fancy; rich, not gaudy;
For the apparel oft proclaims the man;
And they in France of the best rank and station
Are of a most select and generous chief in that.
Neither a borrower, nor a lender be;
For loan oft loses both itself and friend,
And borrowing dulls the edge of husbandry.
This above all: to thine own self be true,
And it must follow, as the night the day,
Thou canst not then be false to any man.
Farewell; my blessing season this in thee!

William Shakespeare (1564–1616)

Trust and obey

The origins of this hymn lay in an evangelistic gathering held in Brockton, Massachusetts, in 1886. When the audience were asked to express their thoughts on salvation one young man rose to share his intention to 'trust and obey' – a sentiment that, when reported to the minister John Sammis, inspired the following verses.

When we walk with the Lord
In the light of His word,
What a glory He sheds on our way!
While we do His good will,
He abides with us still,
And with all who will trust and obey.

Trust and obey,
For there's no other way
To be happy with Jesus,
But to trust and obey.

Not a shadow can rise,
Not a cloud in the skies,
But His smile quickly drives it away;
Not a doubt nor a fear,
Not a sigh nor a tear,
Can abide while we trust and obey.

Not a burden we bear,
Not a sorrow we share,
But our toil He will richly repay;
Not a grief nor a loss,
Not a frown nor a cross,
But is blest if we trust and obey.

But we never can prove
The delights of His love
Until all on the altar we lay;
For the favour He shows,
And the joy He bestows,
Are for them who will trust and obey.

Then in fellowship sweet
We will sit at His feet,
Or we'll walk by His side in the way;
What He says we will do,
Where He sends we will go –
Never fear, only trust and obey.

John H. Sammis (1846–1919)

Turn the other cheek

Several passages in the Bible are devoted to pressing the case for forgiveness of one's enemies. These verses, from Matthew 5:38–42, from Christ's Sermon on the Mount, are perhaps both the most succinct and the most forceful of them all.

You have heard that it was said, 'An eye for an eye and a tooth for a tooth.' But I say to you, Do not resist an evildoer. But if anyone strikes you on the right cheek, turn the other also; and if anyone wants to sue you and take your coat, give your cloak as well; and if anyone forces you to go one mile, go also the second mile. Give to everyone who begs from you, and do not refuse anyone who wants to borrow from you.

Vitaï Lampada

This poem by Henry Newbolt sums up the ethos of the Victorian English gentleman as no other work does, moving effortlessly from the quintessential English game of cricket to the battlefields on which the British Empire was built. Even today it conjures up notions of courage, duty and sportsmanship that many find irresistible.

There's a breathless hush in the Close to-night –
Ten to make and the match to win –
A bumping pitch and a blinding light,
An hour to play and the last man in.
And it's not for the sake of a ribboned coat,
Or the selfish hope of a season's fame,
But his Captain's hand on his shoulder smote –
'Play up! play up! and play the game!'

The sand of the desert is sodden red, –
Red with the wreck of a square that broke; –
The Gatling's jammed and the Colonel dead,
And the regiment blind with dust and smoke.
The river of death has brimmed his banks,
And England's far, and Honour a name,
But the voice of a schoolboy rallies the ranks:
'Play up! play up! and play the game!'

This is the word that year by year,
While in her place the School is set,
Every one of her sons must hear,
And none that hears it dare forget.
This they all with a joyful mind
Bear through life like a torch in flame,
And falling fling to the host behind –
'Play up! play up! and play the game!'

Henry Newbolt (1862–1938)

We brought nothing into this world

This passage, from 1 Timothy 6:1–12, gives Paul's advice to Timothy, recommending a life of dutiful faith rather than one dedicated to the pursuit of material wealth.

Let all who are under the yoke of slavery regard their masters as worthy of all honour, so that the name of God and the teaching may not be blasphemed. Those who have believing masters must not be disrespectful to them on the ground that they are members of the church; rather they must serve them all the more, since those who benefit by their service are believers and beloved. Teach and urge these duties. Whoever teaches otherwise and does not agree with the sound words of our Lord Jesus Christ and the teaching that is in accordance with godliness, is conceited, understanding nothing, and has a morbid craving for controversy and for disputes about words. From these come envy, dissension, slander, base suspicions, and wrangling among those who are depraved in mind and bereft of the truth, imagining that godliness is a means of gain. Of course, there is great gain in godliness combined with contentment; for we brought nothing into the world, so that we can take nothing out of it; but if we have food and clothing, we will be content with these. But those who want to be rich fall into temptation and are trapped by many senseless and harmful desires that plunge people into ruin and destruction. For the love of money is a root of all kinds of evil, and in their eagerness to be rich some have wandered away from the faith and pierced themselves with many pains.

But as for you, man of God, shun all this; pursue righteousness, godliness, faith, love, endurance, gentleness. Fight the good fight of the faith; take hold of the eternal life, to which you were called and for which you made the good confession in the presence of many witnesses.

We plough the fields, and scatter

This hymn, which ranks among the most popular of all harvest songs, is of German origin. It was first sung at a village festival in northern Germany in 1782, based by Matthias Claudius (a journalist and close friend of Goethe) upon a peasant song he had heard at a farm nearby. It was translated into English by music teacher Jane Montgomery Campbell (1817–78) and enjoyed a new lease of life in the 1960s when it was included in the score of the musical Godspell.

We plough the fields, and scatter
The good seed on the land,
But it is fed and watered
By God's almighty hand;
He sends the snow in winter,
The warmth to swell the grain,
The breezes and the sunshine,
And soft refreshing rain:

All good gifts around us
Are sent from heaven above;
Then thank the Lord, O thank the Lord,
For all His love.

He only is the maker
Of all things near and far;
He paints the wayside flower;
He lights the evening star;
The winds and waves obey Him,
By Him the birds are fed;
Much more to us, His children,
He gives our daily bread:

We thank Thee then, O Father,
For all things bright and good,
The seed-time and the harvest,
Our life, our health, our food.
No gifts have we to offer
For all Thy love imparts,
But that which Thou desirest
Our humble, thankful hearts.

Matthias Claudius (1740–1815)

We rest on Thee

This hymn, written by Edith Gilling Cherry, is most often sung to Sibelius' music Finlandia. *In January 1956, five missionaries sang it before entering the Ecuadorian jungle to bring the Gospel to the Auca Indians. After the men reached the Aucas, the Indians murdered them. However, years later, contact with the Aucas was re-established, and many came to Christ, including the killers, which is how first-hand details of the missionaries' deaths came to light.*

We rest on Thee, our Shield and our Defender!
We go not forth alone against the foe;
Strong in Thy strength, safe in Thy keeping tender,
We rest on Thee, and in Thy Name we go.
Strong in Thy strength, safe in Thy keeping tender,
We rest on Thee, and in Thy Name we go.

Yes, in Thy Name, O Captain of salvation!
In Thy dear Name, all other names above;
Jesus our Righteousness, our sure Foundation,
Our Prince of glory and our King of love.
Jesus our Righteousness, our sure Foundation,
Our Prince of glory and our King of love.

We go in faith, our own great weakness feeling,
And needing more each day Thy grace to know:
Yet from our hearts a song of triumph pealing,
'We rest on Thee, and in Thy Name we go.'
Yet from our hearts a song of triumph pealing,
'We rest on Thee, and in Thy Name we go.'

We rest on Thee, our Shield and our Defender!
Thine is the battle, Thine shall be the praise;
When passing through the gates of pearly splendour,
Victors, we rest with Thee, through endless days.
When passing through the gates of pearly splendour,
Victors, we rest with Thee, through endless days.

Edith Gilling Cherry (1872–97)

We shall fight them on the beaches

This speech, made by Prime Minister Winston Churchill on 4 June 1940, was delivered at a time of great national trepidation, when the forces of Nazi Germany were poised to invade the British Isles. It remains one of Churchill's most celebrated wartime speeches and a model for leaders seeking to stiffen national resolve in times of crisis.

I have, myself, full confidence that if all do their duty, if nothing is neglected, and if the best arrangements are made, as they are being made, we shall prove ourselves once again able to defend our Island home, to ride out the storm of war, and to outlive the menace of tyranny, if necessary for years, if necessary alone.

At any rate, that is what we are going to try to do. That is the resolve of His Majesty's Government – every man of them. That is the will of Parliament and the nation.

The British Empire and the French Republic, linked together in their cause and in their need, will defend to the death their native soil, aiding each other like good comrades to the utmost of their strength.

Even though large tracts of Europe and many old and famous States have fallen or may fall into the grip of the Gestapo and all the odious apparatus of Nazi rule, we shall not flag or fail.

We shall go on to the end, we shall fight in France, we shall fight on the seas and oceans, we shall fight with growing confidence and growing strength in the air, we shall defend our Island, whatever the cost may be, we shall fight on the beaches, we shall fight on the landing grounds, we shall fight in the fields and in the streets, we shall fight in the hills; we shall never surrender, and even if, which I do not for a moment believe, this Island or a large part of it were subjugated and starving, then our Empire beyond the seas, armed and guarded by the British Fleet, would carry on the struggle, until, in God's good time, the New World, with all its power and might, steps forth to the rescue and the liberation of the old.

Winston Churchill (1874–1965)

The wedding at Cana

The story of the miracle of the water turned into wine, related at John 2:1–11, remains one of the best-loved episodes in the Bible, showing Christ's power over nature. It is sometimes read at wedding services.

On the third day there was a wedding in Cana of Galilee, and the mother of Jesus was there. Jesus and his disciples had also been invited to the wedding. When the wine gave out, the mother of Jesus said to him, 'They have no wine.' And Jesus said to her, 'Woman, what concern is that to you and to me? My hour has not yet come.' His mother said to the servants, 'Do whatever he tells you.' Now standing there were six stone water-jars for the Jewish rites of purification, each holding twenty or thirty gallons. Jesus said to them, 'Fill the jars with water.' And they filled them up to the brim. He said to them, 'Now draw some out, and take it to the chief steward.' So they took it. When the steward tasted the water that had become wine, and did not know where it came from (though the servants who had drawn the water knew), the steward called the bridegroom and said to him, 'Everyone serves the good wine first, and then the inferior wine after the guests have become drunk. But you have kept the good wine until now.' Jesus did this, the first of his signs, in Cana of Galilee, and revealed his glory; and his disciples believed in him.

Were you there?

This hymn by an unknown author has its origins in the tradition of the American spiritual, hence its repetitive structure and direct appeal to the listener.

Were you there when they crucified my Lord?
Were you there when they crucified my Lord?
Oh, sometimes it causes me to tremble, tremble, tremble;
Were you there when they crucified my Lord?

Were you there when they nailed Him to the tree?
Were you there when they nailed Him to the tree?
Oh, sometimes it causes me to tremble, tremble, tremble;
Were you there when they nailed Him to the tree?

Were you there when they pierced Him in the side?
Were you there when they pierced Him in the side?
Oh, sometimes it causes me to tremble, tremble, tremble;
Were you there when they pierced Him in the side?

Were you there when the sun refused to shine?
Were you there when the sun refused to shine?
Oh, sometimes it causes me to tremble, tremble, tremble;
Were you there when the sun refused to shine?

Were you there when they laid Him in the tomb?
Were you there when they laid Him in the tomb?
Oh, sometimes it causes me to tremble, tremble, tremble;
Were you there when they laid Him in the tomb?

Were you there when God raised Him from the dead?
Were you there when God raised Him from the dead?
Oh, sometimes it causes me to tremble, tremble, tremble;
Were you there when God raised Him from the dead?

Were you there when He ascended up on high?
Were you there when He ascended up on high?
Oh, sometimes it causes me to tremble, tremble, tremble;
Were you there when He ascended up on high?

Anonymous

What a friend we have in Jesus

The life of Joseph Medlicott Scriven, the Irish author of this familiar hymn, was marked with tragedy, adding great poignancy to the following verses. He never enjoyed good health and, as a young man, lost his fiancée the evening before their wedding when she was accidentally drowned. Subsequently he emigrated to Canada and there became engaged once more, only to lose this second bride to illness before they could be married. While still in Canada he received news that his mother was seriously ill back in Ireland. Having nothing else to offer her, he sent her these words of comfort. Scriven himself was found drowned in a pool near Rice Lake in October 1886.

What a friend we have in Jesus,
All our sins and griefs to bear!
What a privilege to carry
Everything to God in prayer!
O what peace we often forfeit,
O what needless pain we bear,
All because we do not carry
Everything to God in prayer!

Have we trials and temptations,
Is there trouble anywhere?
We should never be discouraged:
Take it to the Lord in prayer.
Can we find a friend so faithful
Who will all our sorrows share?
Jesus knows our every weakness:
Take it to the Lord in prayer.

Are we weak and heavy-laden,
Cumbered with a load of care?
Precious Saviour, still our refuge –
Take it to the Lord in prayer.
Do thy friends despise, forsake thee?
Take it to the Lord in prayer;
In His arms He'll take and shield thee,
Thou wilt find a solace there.

Joseph Medlicott Scriven (1819–86)

What is man?

The relative insignificance of human beings in the context of the universe is poignantly expressed in Psalm 8:1–9, which shows the amazing condescension of God in his majesty to care about us mere mortals.

O LORD, our Lord, how excellent is thy name in all the earth! who hast set thy glory above the heavens.

Out of the mouth of babes and sucklings hast thou ordained strength because of thine enemies, that thou mightest still the enemy and the avenger.

When I consider thy heavens, the work of thy fingers, the moon and the stars, which thou hast ordained;

What is man, that thou art mindful of him? and the son of man, that thou visitest him?

For thou hast made him a little lower than the angels, and hast crowned him with glory and honour.

Thou madest him to have dominion over the works of thy hands; thou hast put all things under his feet:

All sheep and oxen, yea, and the beasts of the field,

The fowls of the air, and the fish of the sea, and whatsoever passeth through the paths of the seas.

O LORD, our Lord, how excellent is thy name in all the earth!

(Authorized [King James] Version)

What God has joined together, let no one separate

Lines from this passage, from Mark 10:1–9, are widely familiar from their inclusion in marriage services.

He left that place and went to the region of Judea and beyond the Jordan. And crowds again gathered around him; and, as was his custom, he again taught them.

Some Pharisees came, and to test him they asked, 'Is it lawful for a man to divorce his wife?' He answered them, 'What did Moses command you?' They said, 'Moses allowed a man to write a certificate of dismissal and to divorce her.' But Jesus said to them, 'Because of your hardness of heart he wrote this commandment for you. But from the beginning of creation, "God made them male and female." "For this reason a man shall leave his father and mother and be joined to his wife, and the two shall become one flesh." So they are no longer two, but one flesh. Therefore what God has joined together, let no one separate.'

When I am dead, my dearest

This poem by Christina Rossetti ranks among her most famous work. Typically melancholy in tone, it has yet a consolatory note that has made it a favourite choice of reading at funerals.

When I am dead, my dearest,
Sing no sad songs for me;
Plant thou no roses at my head,
Nor shady cypress tree:
Be the green grass above me
With showers and dewdrops wet;
And if thou wilt, remember,
And if thou wilt, forget.

I shall not see the shadows,
I shall not feel the rain;
I shall not hear the nightingale
Sing on, as if in pain;
And dreaming through the twilight
That doth not rise nor set,
Haply I may remember,
And haply may forget.

Christina Rossetti (1830–94)

When I survey the wondrous cross

This is perhaps the most famous hymn by Isaac Watts, who is sometimes called the 'Father of English Hymnody'. The story goes that Watts took up hymn writing at the tender age of 19 after complaining about the quality of the hymns being sung at the local church and being challenged by his father to do better himself. Other classic productions of his hand include 'O God, our help in ages past' and 'Jesus shall reign where'er the sun'.

When I survey the wondrous cross,
On which the Prince of glory died,
My richest gain I count but loss,
And pour contempt on all my pride.

Forbid it, Lord, that I should boast,
Save in the death of Christ my God;
All the vain things that charm me most,
I sacrifice them to His blood.

See from His head, His hands, His feet,
Sorrow and love flow mingled down;
Did e'er such love and sorrow meet,
Or thorns compose so rich a crown?

His dying crimson, like a robe,
Spreads o'er His body on the tree;
Then am I dead to all the globe,
And all the globe is dead to me.

Were the whole realm of nature mine,
That were a present far too small;
Love so amazing, so divine,
Demands my soul, my life, my all.

Isaac Watts (1674–1748)

When my hour is come

The Irish writer and artist George William Russell, who published books under the pseudonym A.E., interested himself in many fields of human enterprise from art to political economics. This poem, in which he contemplates his own death, testifies to his interest in mysticism, which was promoted by his friendship with fellow-poet W. B. Yeats and the so-called theosophists.

When my hour is come
Let no teardrop fall
And no darkness hover
Round me where I lie.
Let the vastness call
One who was its lover,
Let me breathe the sky.

Where the lordly light
Walks along the world,
And its silent tread
Leaves the grasses bright,
Leaves the flowers uncurled,
Let me to the dead
Breathe a gay goodnight.

George William Russell (1867–1935)

Where you go I will go

The biblical story of Ruth and Naomi is related at Ruth 1:11–19. Ruth demonstrates her love for her mother-in-law Naomi by refusing to be parted from her after the death of her husband, Naomi's son, even though this means Ruth will lose her chance to marry again. The story is a shining example of family devotion and self-sacrifice.

But Naomi said, 'Turn back, my daughters, why will you go with me? Do I still have sons in my womb that they may become your husbands? Turn back, my daughters, go your way, for I am too old to have a husband. Even if I thought there was hope for me, even if I should have a husband tonight and bear sons, would you then wait until they were grown? Would you then refrain from marrying? No, my daughters, it has been far more bitter for me than for you, because the hand of the LORD has turned against me.' Then they wept aloud again. Orpah kissed her mother-in-law, but Ruth clung to her.

So she said, 'See, your sister-in-law has gone back to her people and to her gods; return after your sister-in-law.' But Ruth said,

'Do not press me to leave you
    or to turn back from following you!
Where you go, I will go;
    where you lodge, I will lodge;
your people shall be my people,
    and your God my God.

Where you die, I will die – there will I be buried. May the LORD do thus and so to me, and more as well, if even death parts me from you!'

When Naomi saw that she was determined to go with her, she said no more to her. So the two of them went on until they came to Bethlehem. When they came to Bethlehem, the whole town was stirred because of them; and the women said, 'Is this Naomi?'

While shepherds watched their flocks by night

This has long been one of the most popular of all Christmas carols. These familiar verses by Poet Laureate Nahum Tate did not, however, appear in the celebrated 'New Version' of the Psalter published by Tate and Nicholas Brady in 1696 but were among the supplement of 16 new hymns added in 1700.

While shepherds watched their flocks by night,
All seated on the ground,
The angel of the Lord came down,
And glory shone around.

'Fear not,' said he (for mighty dread
Had seized their troubled mind),
'Glad tidings of great joy I bring
To you and all mankind.

'To you in David's town this day
Is born of David's line
A Saviour, who is Christ the Lord;
And this shall be the sign:

'The heavenly Babe you there shall find
To human view displayed,
All meanly wrapped in swathing-bands,
And in a manger laid.'

Thus spake the seraph; and forthwith
Appeared a shining throng
Of angels, praising God, who thus
Addressed their joyful song:

'All glory be to God on high,
And to the world be peace!
Goodwill henceforth from heaven to earth
Begin and never cease!'

Nahum Tate (1652–1715)

Who will separate us from the love of Christ?

These verses, from Romans 8:31–39, give support to the idea that nothing can ultimately prevail against the truly faithful: if God is on your side, no enemy need be feared.

What then are we to say about these things? If God is for us, who is against us? He who did not withhold his own Son, but gave him up for all of us, will he not with him also give us everything else? Who will bring any charge against God's elect? It is God who justifies. Who is to condemn? It is Christ Jesus, who died, yes, who was raised, who is at the right hand of God, who indeed intercedes for us. Who will separate us from the love of Christ? Will hardship, or distress, or persecution, or famine, or nakedness, or peril, or sword? As it is written,

'For your sake we are being killed all day long;
we are accounted as sheep to be slaughtered.'

No, in all these things we are more than conquerors through him who loved us. For I am convinced that neither death, nor life, nor angels, nor rulers, nor things present, nor things to come, nor powers, nor height, nor depth, nor anything else in all creation, will be able to separate us from the love of God in Christ Jesus our Lord.

Who would true valour see

These lines come from the end of Part 2 of Pilgrim's Progress *(1684) by the celebrated Protestant tinker poet John Bunyan. They were adapted by Dr Percy Dearmer in the* English Hymnal *published in 1906 and it is this version that is usually sung today, the first line often changed to 'He who would valiant be'. The accompanying tune is Vaughan Williams' 'Monk's Gate'.*

Who would true valour see,
Let him come hither;
One here will constant be,
Come wind, come weather.
There's no discouragement
Shall make him once relent
His first avow'd intent,
To be a pilgrim.

Whoso beset him round
With dismal stories,
Do but themselves confound,
His strength the more is.
No lion can him fright,
He'll with a giant fight,
But he will have a right
To be a pilgrim.

Hobgoblin, nor foul fiend,
Can daunt his spirit;
He knows, he at the end
Shall life inherit.
Then fancies fly away,
He'll fear not what men say,
He'll labour night and day
To be a pilgrim.

John Bunyan (1628–88)

Whoever welcomes one such child

This passage from Mark 9:33–37 reinforces the belief that children have a special place in Christ's affections. Here the childish behaviour of the disciples as they argue and then sullenly refuse to say what they have been arguing about is highlighted by the introduction of an actual child, with Christ's acceptance and care of the child indicating the response required of all Christ's followers.

Then they came to Capernaum; and when he was in the house he asked them, 'What were you arguing about on the way?' But they were silent, for on the way they had argued with one another about who was the greatest. He sat down, called the twelve, and said to them, 'Whoever wants to be first must be last of all and servant of all.' Then he took a little child and put it among them; and taking it in his arms, he said to them, 'Whoever welcomes one such child in my name welcomes me, and whoever welcomes me welcomes not me but the one who sent me.'

Wives and husbands

This passage from Ephesians 5:21-33 is sometimes used as a Bible reading at weddings. It stresses the mutual and reciprocal relationship of love and respect within marriage. Marriage is an illustration of the relationship between Christ and his church. It is a precious union that needs caring, self-sacrificing love.

Be subject to one another out of reverence for Christ. Wives, be subject to your husbands as you are to the Lord. For the husband is the head of the wife just as Christ is the head of the church, the body of which he is the Saviour. Just as the church is subject to Christ, so also wives ought to be, in everything, to their husbands.

Husbands, love your wives, just as Christ loved the church and gave himself up for her, in order to make her holy by cleansing her with the washing of water by the word, so as to present the church to himself in splendour, without a spot or wrinkle or anything of the kind – yes, so that she may be holy and without blemish. In the same way, husbands should love their wives as they do their own bodies. He who loves his wife loves himself. For no one ever hates his own body, but he nourishes and tenderly cares for it, just as Christ does for the church, because we are members of his body. 'For this reason a man will leave his father and mother and be joined to his wife, and the two will become one flesh.' This is a great mystery, and I am applying it to Christ and the church. Each of you, however, should love his wife as himself, and a wife should respect her husband.

The wolf shall live with the lamb

This passage from Isaiah 11:6–9 encapsulates the concept of reconciliation and the triumph of peace-making over violence. It is frequently cited in situations of conflict in the hope of achieving a resolution of differences.

The wolf shall live with the lamb,
the leopard shall lie down with the kid,
the calf and the lion and the fatling together,
and a little child shall lead them.
The cow and the bear shall graze,
their young shall lie down together;
and the lion shall eat straw like the ox.
The nursing child shall play over the hole of the asp,
and the weaned child shall put its hand on the adder's den.
They will not hurt or destroy
on all my holy mountain;
for the earth will be full of the knowledge of the LORD
as the waters cover the sea.

The Word became flesh

This passage from John 1:1–14, in which St John unfolds the great mystery of the incarnation, is traditionally read as the ninth lesson in the Christmas Eve service of nine lessons and carols. The most well known of these services is held every year at King's College Chapel, Cambridge, from where it is broadcast all over the world.

In the beginning was the Word, and the Word was with God, and the Word was God. He was in the beginning with God. All things came into being through him, and without him not one thing came into being. What has come into being in him was life, and the life was the light of all people. The light shines in the darkness, and the darkness did not overcome it.

There was a man sent from God, whose name was John. He came as a witness to testify to the light, so that all might believe through him. He himself was not the light, but he came to testify to the light. The true light, which enlightens everyone, was coming into the world.

He was in the world, and the world came into being through him; yet the world did not know him. He came to what was his own, and his own people did not accept him. But to all who received him, who believed in his name, he gave power to become children of God, who were born, not of blood or of the will of the flesh or of the will of man, but of God.

And the Word became flesh and lived among us, and we have seen his glory, the glory as of a father's only son, full of grace and truth.

Acknowledgements

Blood, toil, tears and sweat Reproduced with permission of Curtis Brown Ltd, London on behalf of The Estate of Sir Winston S. Churchill © Winston S. Churchill

Christ triumphant Words: © Michael Saward/Jubilate Hymns, used by permission

The Lake isle of Innisfree Reproduced with permission of A.P Watt Ltd on behalf of Michael B Yeats

Lord of all hopefulness Words by Jan Struther (1901-53) from 'Enlarged Songs of Praise 1931' by permission of Oxford University Press

Make me a channel of your peace Dedicated to Mrs. Frances Tracy. © 1967, OCP Publications, 5536NE Hassalo, Portland, OR97213. All rights reserved. Used with permission

They shall not grow old The Society of Authors as the Literary Representative of the Estate of Laurence Binyon

Thine be the glory By permission of the World Student Christian Federation

We shall fight them on the beaches Reproduced with permission of Curtis Brown Ltd, London on behalf of The Estate of Sir Winston S. Churchill © Winston S. Churchill